Mel Bay Presents

Learn To Play
Fingerstyle Solos
for 'UKULELE

By
Mark
Kailana
Nelson

D1225013

Cover Credit: Custom Koa Tenor 'Ukulele by Po Mahina, Na'alehu, HI – Dennis Lake, luthier.
Photo by Helga Motley

CD CONTENTS

MEL BAY

1 2 3 4 5 6 7 8 9 0

Visit us on the Web at www.melbay.com — E-mail us at email@melbay.com

Foreword

I suppose I could make some claim to having played the 'ukulele for 50 years. After all, I do remember dinking away on one my parents brought back from Hawai'i in the early '50s. And then there was the time in grade school when we all learned to dance and sing "we're going to a hukilau." In fact, it seems there was always a 'ukulele around when I was growing up. But, to tell the truth, I never really got serious about the instrument until quite recently, when I began hosting the Aloha Music Camp with famed Hawaiian musician Keola Beamer.

Shortly before our first camp, a friend fished a battered uke out of the trash and gave it to me. I strung it up and tossed it in my luggage, thinking maybe someone would want to borrow it. That someone turned out to be my wife Annie, who in 25 years of marriage had never expressed the slightest desire to play a musical instrument. You can imagine my surprise and delight when she not only faithfully attended the daily classes, but even performed in the student show!

This was what drew me in: here was an instrument that could be easily learned, didn't make a huge dent in your wallet, and brought smiles to the faces of every one who held one. As someone who has devoted his entire life to helping people to play music, I had to learn more.

Through the Aloha Music Camp I have been able to meet and study with some of Hawaii's finest 'ukulele players and teachers: Herb Ohta, Jr.; Keoki Kahumoku; the incomparable Byron Yasui and the "'Ukulele Lady" herself: Cindy Combs. They showed me that it was possible to go beyond the "doo-wacka-doo" silliness so often associated on the mainland with this most Hawaiian of musical instruments. And they inspired me to apply my skills as a guitarist – how to weave intricate fingerstyle arrangements – to this little four stringed guitar.

This book is the result. The music comes from all over – I wanted to present both the familiar and exotic. And who's to say which is which? If you live in Des Moines, Hawaiian songs like "Ahi Wela" and "E Ku'u Morning Dew" may be new to you, but every child of the Islands knows them by heart. Likewise, a mother in Honolulu may be delighted to discover that the Welsh/Appalachian lullaby "All Through the Night" is the perfect song to send her baby into dreamland.

I hope you find as much enjoyment in playing these songs on your 'ukulele as I do. After all, like they say, "Four strings, four fingers…no problem!"

Mark Kailana Nelson & Annie Lanamalie Dempsey,
Aloha Music Camp 2001.
Photo by Arna

Table of Contents

* Arrangements that may be played on Baritone 'ukulele or instruments with low G strings.

About the Book

For an instrument that's only been around since the 1880s, the 'ukulele has developed a number of forms and tunings. On the mainland, most people play in one of two tunings: G-C-E-A (starting on the fourth string) or the slightly higher "East Coast tuning": A-D-F♯-B. Although this book is written for a soprano, concert or tenor uke in G-C-E-A tuning, you can play all of the arrangements in the higher tuning simply by following the TAB. If you don't know how to read TAB, see the next section.

In Hawai'i, where the G-C-E-A tuning is standard, you'll often find six- and eight-stringed instruments, which are wonderful for chording and create a nice tinkling sound when picked. Many Island players use a low G string to extend the range – handy when playing melodies and leads. Some of these arrangements will work equally well for instruments with high or low G's. The exceptions, such as the Bach "Minuet" and "Somewhere Over the Rainbow," feature melody notes that take advantage of the standard reentrant tuning. Similarly, baritone players will have to pick and choose. I've indicated arrangements that may be played on baritones and ukes with low G tunings in the Table of Contents.

The book was designed for intermediate 'ukulele players, though dedicated beginners can and should use it to progress beyond simple strums. By "intermediate," I mean that you already know how to play a number of songs using basic chords, you have a few strums under your fingers, and you are ready to move ahead into playing chords and melody up the neck. No matter what your skill level, a little time spent practicing the chord inversions starting on page 91 will greatly enhance your enjoyment.

The book is arranged in two sections. First comes some basic introductory material about reading music and tablature and a lesson in fingerpicking. If you already know how, feel free to skip directly to the arrangements. These are given in increasing levels of difficulty: a group of six fairly easy arrangements within the reach of most advancing 'ukulele players, followed by a half dozen slightly more challenging arrangements. The final grouping has more difficult arrangements featuring uncommon chord forms, tricky fingerings and all the fun stuff I could muster.

Although you can play these arrangements on any 'ukulele, players with larger hands might want to pick up a tenor. The longer scale and slightly wider fingerboard allow you room for your fingers. What's more, many soprano and concert sized instruments stop at the 14th fret, which limits the range considerably.

Of course, feel free to play these on any instrument you have on hand. I love playing "Mbube" on my 6 string; the octave strings lend a great fullness to the picking patterns. Likewise, the two blues songs sound great on a banjo-uke or resonator instrument.

Above all – take it slow and enjoy the music.

Mahalo nui loa to Dennis Lake for his incredible craftsmanship; to the Beamer *'ohana* for teaching me the true spirit of aloha; to William Bay and Mel Bay Publications for continued support over the years; to Annie, for writing both the song *and* the key; and to all 'ukulele players everywhere, for showing just how much fun you can have with four strings.
All photos by the author.

Part One ~ Getting Started

This section covers the basics of reading Tablature and musical notation and offers a lesson on how to play fingerstyle 'ukulele. And you'll have a chance to develop your technique on that great Hawaiian lullaby "'Imo 'Imo Hoku Iki" – better known as "Twinkle Twinkle Little Star." Use this material to get you prepared for the more challenging material presented later.

A collection of classic Hawaiian songbooks.

Reading Musical Notation & Tablature

Although it is not necessary to know how to read musical notation to play the songs in this book, knowledge of a few musical symbols will greatly enhance your enjoyment.

Since the TAB will give you the correct pitches on a properly tuned 'ukulele, you really only have to worry about the rhythm of a particular piece.

Music is divided into **measures**, each of which contains the number of beats delineated by the **time signature:**

 4/4 means four beats per measure, each quarter note counts as 1 beat.

 3/4 is three beats per measure, each quarter note counts as 1 beat.

 6/8 has six beats per measure, with an eighth note getting the beat.

Occasionally alternate symbols are used for the time signature. **Cut Time (¢)** is another way of writing 2/2; and **Common Time (C)** is the same as 4/4.

Each beat can be further divided into smaller and smaller units:

o   The longest note is the whole note; it is the equivalent of four quarter notes, or four counts.

The half note is equal to two quarter notes.

The quarter note gets one count.

Two eighth notes equal a quarter note.

The sixteenth note is half as long as the eighth note; so two sixteenths equal one eighth, four sixteenths equal a quarter, and sixteen equal a whole note.

Rests correspond to each of the different note values.

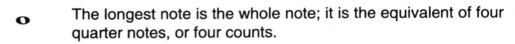

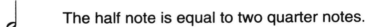

A dot placed next to a note (or rest) lengthens it by one half of its value. For example:

Ties are used for notes that are held for their combined values:

This figure would be held as long as three eighth notes.

Triplets are groups of three notes that are played in the space of two.

For example, three eighth note triplets

would be played in the same amount of time as two eighth notes:

Repeat signs: repeat the enclosed phrase one time before going on to the next measure. (Note that often the first section of a song only has the sign at the end of the phrase. This is a convention of writing folk tunes; treat it just as if the first sign was there.)

This sign means play the measures under the sign on the first time through and then go back to the beginning of the section. On the repeat you skip over the first ending and play the second ending.

D.C.

From the Italian, **Da Capo**, meaning "Head." This sign directs you to go back to the beginning of the music.

D.S.

Dal Segno, or "to the sign," tells you to look for the symbol (𝄋) and play that section next rather than returning to the beginning.

The **Coda**, Italian for "tail," is the ending section. When you see the phase *To Coda*, skip ahead to the section marked with this symbol.

A **fermata** is the symbol to hold a note just a little longer than its value. It is used to add expression to your playing.

Chord symbols are given for all of the songs; these may be played on a second 'ukulele, guitar, etc. What's more, the chord symbols can be useful to help you determine the correct fingering for a musical passage. Remember that the chords used often represent one of several alternative harmonies to the melody; feel free to change them if you'd like.

Tablature, or TAB is actually far older than "standard" musical notation. In tablature, the four strings of your instrument are represented as lines. The line at the top is the first, or A string and the G string is on the bottom. It's almost as if you were looking at your instrument upside down!

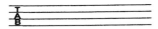

Numbers on the lines tell you where to place your fingers. In the example below, play the first string at the 3rd fret followed by the second string at the 5th fret:

Open strings are indicated by a zero. Here's what a basic F chord looks like in TAB:

Although TAB doesn't give you the rhythmic values of the notes (for that, refer to the notation), you can get an idea of when to play a given note by its relative position. In this example, play the two notes on the 2nd & 4th strings simultaneously, followed by the open 1st and 3rd strings:

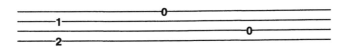

Right hand fingerings have not been indicated to allow each player to develop a personal style – experiment with different fingering to see which works best for you. In many of the arrangements, the Performance Notes section offers suggestions. For the most part, I favor using my thumb and three fingers, placed one per string.

Here are some more TAB symbols you will encounter:

Slide Pick the first note, then slide up or down to the next. Try to sound each note cleanly. The second example features a double stop slide.

Sometimes you'll see a slide like this:

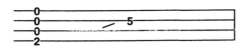

This means to quickly slide into the note from some place lower down the neck, it really doesn't matter where. You can also do a slide down to let the note "fall off."

Hammer-on Play the first note, then "hammer" your finger down to the fingerboard to sound the second note. You can hammer-on from an open string, or from any fret to any higher note.

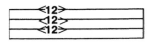

Pull-off The opposite of a hammer-on. Play the first note, then quickly pull your finger off the fretboard to play the second note. Some people find these difficult. Don't be tempted to pluck the string sideways – instead try to catch the string in the meat of your finger as you lift it off.

Harmonics Lightly touch the string or strings directly over the fret to produce a ringing tone. Unlike fretting, do not press the string down to the fingerboard, rather rest your finger directly over the top of the fret. As soon as you hear the harmonic, lift your finger to let the tone blossom. Try moving your plucking hand back toward the bridge slightly to better define the harmonic.

Chords and chord diagrams

Most of the arrangements use standard 'ukulele chord shapes, at least as a starting point. I give fingering hints and block chord diagrams in the Performance Notes, but it helps to be familiar with at least the basic major, minor and dominant seventh chords. (See pages 91 - 95).

You can usually figure out the correct chord fingering by looking ahead in the measure and mentally "collapsing" the notes. For example, this measure would be played while holding down a basic D7 chord:

Lastly, while the subject of harmony is well beyond the scope of this book, some of the arrangements make use of fairly sophisticated chords and idiosyncratic harmony choices. Don't worry about the fancy names – and, yes, there are several ways to name the same chord "grip" – just play through the tab and see what comes out. I take full responsibility for any harm that may be done to the folklorically sensitive.

How to Play Fingerstyle 'Ukulele

Since the 'ukulele has been played using the fingers almost exclusively since its earliest development, what exactly is meant by the term "fingerstyle" or "fingerpicking?" A quick poll of the participants at any modern 'ukulele festival reveals a huge variety of finger techniques to sound the strings – strums using the thumb, strums with the fingers, strums with the thumb and fingers – even some players using a large felt flat pick like the one that came with the souvenir uke my parents brought back from Hawai'i in the 50's. And yes, you'll even find some who play melody with one or more of their fingers. So how is "fingerpicking" different?

For the purposes of this book, I define fingerpicking as using your right (or left) hand thumb and fingers to play both melody and accompaniment at the same time. The term comes from folk guitar styles such as the country blues of Mississippi John Hurt and Hawaii's great slack key guitar tradition. Often your thumb will keep up a basic pattern while you add melody and harmony notes with your fingers. Other times you'll alternate full chords with melody notes, or play simple harmonies on two strings. It is a wonderful way to play your instrument with or without accompaniment.

In this part of the book I'll present some lessons and exercises aimed at getting you up to speed playing fingerpicking solos on your 'ukulele. So if you've studied classical guitar, or folk guitar styles such as Travis-picking or slack key, feel free to skip ahead directly to the arrangements.

Example 1 is a simple major scale in the key of F. Play the initial chord with your thumb on the 4th string, index on the 3rd, and middle on the 2nd. Pluck all three strings at the same time, then pick each note, going up the octave. Use your index and middle fingers alternately to play the notes of the scale. Try to hold the chord as long as it's practical.

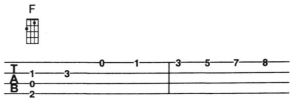

Next, we'll move down the scale. Start with an F chord barred at the 5th fret, with your thumb on the 4th string, index on the 3rd, and middle on the 2nd and ring finger on the 1st. Once again, play as much as you can while holding down the chord – this will help you learn to play melodies and chords at the same time.

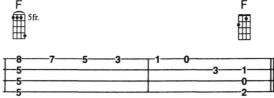

Now try playing up and down the scale without stopping:

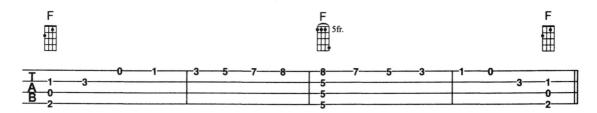

Here's the same scale using a chord for each note. Once again, try playing with your thumb and three fingers of your picking hand. There are many ways to harmonize scales, this one uses basic tonic, subdominant and dominant 7th chords. Notice that in this example chords fall in slightly different places when the scale comes back down:

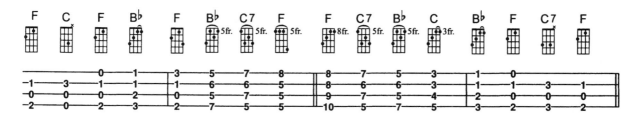

Next we'll do the same thing with a G major scale. You will have to play just part of the G chord for the first and last notes. The chord at the top of the scale may look familiar – it's the same fingering as the F chord you used in the previous example, moved two frets higher.

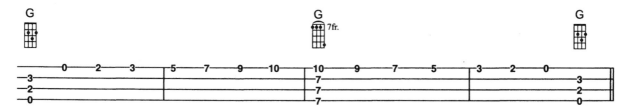

And again, with tonic, subdominant and dominant 7th chords. Notice the alternative chord fingerings for some C and G chords. There's more than one way to skin a cat!

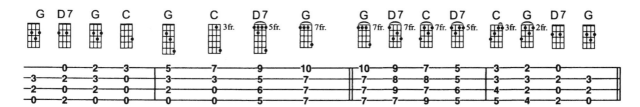

Finally, here's two octaves of a C major scale, starting on the lowest string on your instrument.

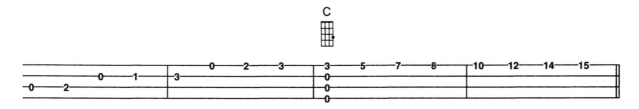

Here's the same scale with some harmony thrown in. Rather than go all the way up to the 15th fret, I just gave you a partial scale for the upper octave.

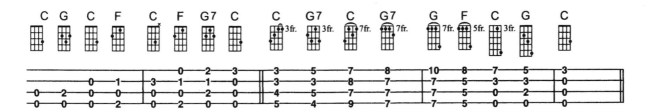

Twinkle Twinkle Little Star

Now that you've played through some of these exercises, let's tackle our first arrangement: "Twinkle Twinkle Little Star." In this and the next example, I have included block chord diagrams to help you find the proper fingering. Remember to play as many notes out of the chord position as you can.

To get started, place your thumb on the 4th string and use one finger per string. For more expressiveness, pluck the chords in a quick rolling motion, starting with your thumb.

The two-note "double stops" on the downbeat of measures 2 & 10 are played as pinches with your thumb and ring finger. Sometimes it is easier to play only part of a chord.

Practice playing the entire piece slowly – try to find a tempo that allows you to play it all the way through without errors.

Next let's look at a more complex arrangement of the same song. This version uses several common fingerpicking patterns, hammer-ons, pulls-offs, slides, double stops and barre chords up the neck – just about every technique you'll encounter in this book is found in this short example! So take it slowly and work on each section until you can play it smoothly. I guarantee that once you can play this up to speed, the rest of the book will be a piece of cake.

Twinkle Twinkle Little Star

Fingerpicking exercises

Refer to the performance notes on the following page for specific tips and suggestions.

Performance Notes

Measure 1: Start out just as you did the last time, then play each note individually moving from string to string. For the second half of the measure, the pattern changes slightly.

Measure 2: Play the first half of the measure while holding down a B♭ chord. It's an unusual fingering, so be careful you don't sound the open C string by mistake:

Measure 4: Play the hammer-on by plucking the open string and then bringing your finger down sharply onto the 2nd fret. Be sure that each note sounds for its full time value.

Measure 5: Play the downbeat as a pinch with your thumb and ring finger and then play strings 2, 3 & 1 with one finger per string while holding down an F chord. Then do exactly the same thing for the B♭ chord. This is one of many common finger picking patterns I've strewn throughout this arrangement.

Measure 7: Another common fingerpicking pattern. Play each chord with your thumb and three fingers, then simply play each string one at a time, starting with your index finger, then middle finger and finally the ring finger.

Measure 8: After you play the C7 on beat 3, quickly move up to the 5th fret and play the double stop, then slide it back down to fret 3.

Measure 9: Here's another typical fingerpicking pattern. Sometimes called "Travis Picking" or "Thumb Picking," it uses an alternating thumb pattern on the 3rd and 4th strings while your index and middle fingers play strings 2 and 3. Because of the high G string, this gives a tinkling "music box" sound. Play the double stops as pinches, and keep your thumb moving. Use a basic F chord, and reach up to the 3rd fret with your pinky.

This is another pattern that is used throughout this book, so take some time to get it right.

Measure 10: Play the B♭ chord using a barre at the 5th fret. Reach up to the 8th fret with your pinky, then pull off back to the 5th fret. Make sure that each note rings clearly – pulling off out of a chord position may take some practice.

Hold the barre to play the partial F chord.

Measure 12: Gradually slow down as you bring the song to a restful conclusion.

As you play through this arrangement, make note of which passages give you trouble and which are easy. Make up exercises to help you get control of your fingers – for instance, you might play measure 1 over and over until you are comfortable, and then add measure 2 and play both of them before adding measure three. Or find a picking pattern that you like and practice it as you play all of the chords in the song.

That concludes the lesson. Let's get started playing some great finger style solos for 'ukulele!

Part Two ~ The Arrangements

The 26 songs are arranged in more or less increasing order of difficulty. First comes a half dozen fairly basic arrangements to get you started, build up your skills and increase your repertoire. These include some classic Hawaiian songs, such as "Pua Sadinia" and "Aloha 'Oe," as well as a couple of folk standards. In order to help you understand how to make your own fingerstyle arrangements, three of the songs appear twice – first in a basic arrangement and later more fully fleshed out.

Next are songs that expand on the techniques covered in the previous section. Here you'll encounter songs that use alternate chord voicings, some new fingerpicking patterns, barre chords moving up the neck and more.

Some of the more demanding techniques include alternate string thumb-picking, used extensively on the bluesy "New Spanish Fandango" and a syncopated version of the steel guitar standard "Hilo March," the slack key style slides of "E Ku'u Morning Dew" and the multiple alternate chord voicings of "Donna Nobis Pacem" and "Danny Boy."

As you work your way towards the back of the book, the arrangements become more challenging, and the technical notes briefer. I've included a handful of my own songs that really give your 'ukulele a workout. I don't intend these arrangements to be set in stone – rather I hope you use them as tools to further your understanding.

I strove to include a fair number of arrangements at each level of difficulty – one of my pet peeves when learning a new style is the dearth of material to practice at each "plateau." Of course, your mileage may vary, so feel free to skip around. To really get the most out of this book, go back and apply the new techniques you've learned to the basic arrangements. It's only when music gets off of the page and into your fingers that it really begins to live.

Six string "Lili'u" tenor 'ukulele.

All Through the Night

Traditional Welsh

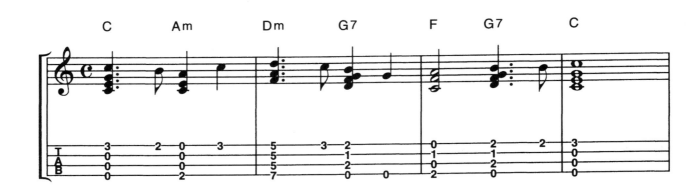

Performance Notes

Originally from Wales, where it is known as *Ar Hyd y Nos*, "All Through the Night" is well loved throughout the British Isles. It is also a favorite lullaby in the Appalachian Mountains.

This fairly simple arrangement is intended to give you practice playing major and minor chords – later on we'll look at the same song again and add some arpeggios, picking patterns, and more complex chords.

You can use just about any picking technique you choose. Playing all of the chords as a slow down stroke with your thumb is very beautiful. In that case, you'd pick any notes on the first string with your index finger. Alternately, try playing each chord as a pinch with your thumb and three fingers. Practicing different picking methods on simple arrangements such as this will help you develop your technique.

Measure 2: Play the Dm chord with a barre on the 5th fret. The G on beat 4 could just as easily been placed on the 2nd string, 3rd fret. But playing on the open string lets it ring out more.

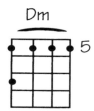

Measures 9 & 10: Play the F chord using a barre at the 5th fret. Then pick each melody note as you go up and back down the scale. Most 'ukulele have position markers at the 10th fret; many also have markers at the 12th fret, so you don't have to count! Be sure to let each note ring for its full time value.

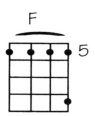

Measure 12: Just another way to play a C chord. Easy, isn't it?

Once you have played through this arrangement, try playing through all the chords using one of the fingerpicking patterns you learned in the lesson.

Las Mañanitas

Traditional Mexican

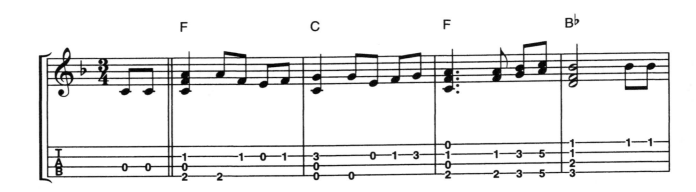

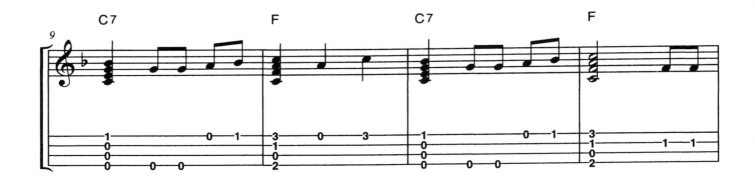

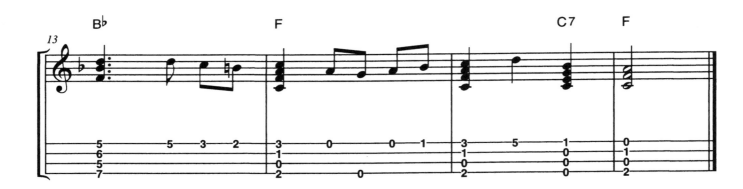

Performance Notes

Throughout Mexico and the Southwest, "Las Mañanitas" is sung early in the morning to begin a child's birthday celebration. It has a lovely melody, and deserves to be more widely known.

This arrangement will help you get used to combining chords, melody notes and double stops. There are several ways to approach picking the chords: I favor placing my thumb on the 4th string, my index on the 3rd string, middle on the 2nd and ring on the 1st. I then pluck the chord with a quick rolling motion starting with my thumb. Some people prefer playing all of the chords as downward strums with the thumb. The choice is yours.

Measure 1: Sound the chord, then use your thumb to play the note on the 4th string (beat 2). Try to hold the chord position while you play the run on the 2nd string. You'll be doing this kind of thing a lot — maintaining the chord position lets the notes ring out and adds a subtle smoothness to your playing.

Measure 3: Play the double stops as pinches with your thumb and index finger.

Measure 6: The melody note – a G – is the sixth of a B♭ chord. Although the chord played on beat 1 is actually a Gm triad, the chord is notated as a B♭ for the purpose of accompaniment.

Measure 13: Play the B♭ chord using a barre on the 5th fret:

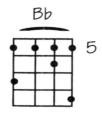

Measure 14: Let go of the F chord after beat 1 to play the melody notes on the 1st and 4th strings.

E Ku'u Morning Dew

Eddie Kamae

Performance Notes

'Ukulele virtuoso Eddie Kamae is one of the most influential Hawaiian musicians of all time. His groundbreaking group, The Sons of Hawaii (which included the legendary slack key guitarist Gabby Pahinui), remains active after almost 40 years. Kamae is notable for researching and reintroducing traditional Hawaiian music and songs to a wider public. His beautiful song, "E Ku'u Morning Dew" ("My Morning Dew"), has become a Hawaiian standard.

This slightly challenging arrangement stays close to the melody — later we'll look at a slack key style treatment of the same song. Play the song slowly and let each chord ring out. This is a good candidate for an old-time style of playing: play the chords and any notes on the 4th string as down strokes with your thumb and use your index finger for all of the melody notes.

Measure 2: Try to make each note of the slide sound for its full value.

Measure 3: Play the C^{sus} & F chords with a gentle strum, slightly quieter than the chord on the downbeat.

Measure 5: Move up to a G chord barred at the 7th fret to play the notes on beats 4:

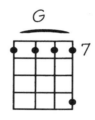

Measure 6: Same trick, different direction. Play the last two notes of the measure from a barre at the 5th fret. Using chord positions like this helps give your playing that sweet legato feel that the Hawaiians call *nahenahe*.

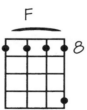

Measure 11: A variation of the lick from measure 3. This time the F chord fills in for the C^{sus} chord.

Measures 15 & 16: This is the first ending, go back to the beginning and play from the repeat sign. On the second pass, skip this measure and play the second ending. Measure 15 features another version of the lick using a suspended chord to fill out the measure.

Measure 18: This lick is one version of the classic Hawaiian turnaround. You'll meet a lot more of these as you work through the arrangements in this book. Let each note ring as you gradually bring the song to a restful conclusion.

Pua Sadinia

David Nape

Performance Notes

In the lovely "Pua Sadinia," the composer compares his beloved to the sweet-smelling gardenia blossom. Although the Hawaiian language does not include the letter "s," it is not uncommon to find it used in words borrowed from English.

This easy arrangement uses only a few barre chords. I leave the picking hand fingering up to you — there are many ways to play this. For a traditional sound, try a downward strum with your thumb for all of the chords, using your index finger to play melody notes on strings 1 and 2 and your thumb for melody on strings 3 and 4. Play the song slowly, and let each note ring out as long as you can. Try to imagine the scent of tropical flowers wafted on soft afternoon trade winds...

Measure 2: Don't be put off by the fancy names — the chords are quite easy to play. The chord on beat 1 is a G^{sus} instead of a C chord to harmonize with the melody note. Likewise, the chord on beat 3 suspends an A (the second) in an G7. Suspended chords bring a wonderful sense of floating to the arrangement, and are used quite a bit in Hawaiian music.

Measure 3: You may be familiar with this chord shape as an Am. Same notes, different name.

Measure 5: Because of the reentrant tuning, where the 4th string is tuned higher than the 2nd or 3rd, sometimes the harmony notes on the G string compete with the melody for attention. Play the double stop on beat one so that the lower of the two notes sounds slightly louder than the high A on the fourth string.

Measure 9: This is the same chord as in measure 1, only voiced with the third doubled instead of the root. The easiest way to play it is with a barre at the 2nd fret. Barre chords are useful because they are easily moved up or down the neck - you'll find this same fingering used again and again in this book.

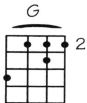

G

Measure 16: Go back to the top and start over. Try to vary the chords or the picking patterns to create your own variations. For example, instead of the G^{sus} and C6 chords in measure 2, how would the melody sound harmonized with an Am7 chord?

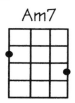

Am7

Measures 17 & 18: Here's another typical Hawaiian turnaround to bring the song to a close. Notice that the final chords are simply two ways of playing the same thing.

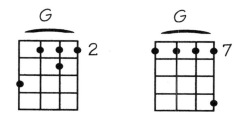

G   G

Isa Lei

Traditional Fijian

Performance Notes

"Isa Lei" is a lovely song of farewell from Fiji. There are numerous sets of lyrics, some modern, some not so. It has been recorded many times, including a lovely slack key rendition by the great Gabby Pahinui. Later we'll take a look at an arrangement that uses some slack key style tricks, but first let's practice playing the basics.

Pickup Measure: Pluck the open 2nd string, then sound the hammer-on by bringing your index finger sharply down to the 1st fret. Be sure to let each note sound for its full time value.

Measure 2: On beat 4, quickly grab an F chord barred at the 5th fret.

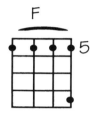

Measure 4: This is the first ending, go back to the beginning and play through to the second ending at measure 5.

Measure 6: Try to play this entire measure while holding down the F chord.

Measure 8: Play the pull-off by plucking the fretted string, and then pulling your finger off the fretboard to sound the open string.

Measure 11: I play the double stops as pinches with my thumb and index finger. Alternately, you may use your index and middle fingers – this sets you up for the three string chord fragment at the top of the next measure.

Measure 12: Play the slide as a smooth transition between frets 3 and 5.

Aloha 'Oe

Queen Lili'uokalani

Track #7

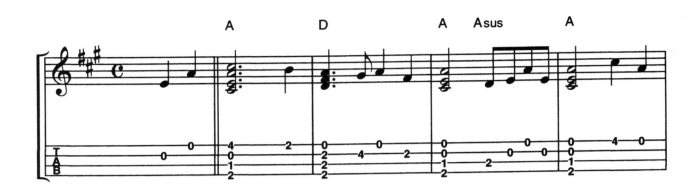

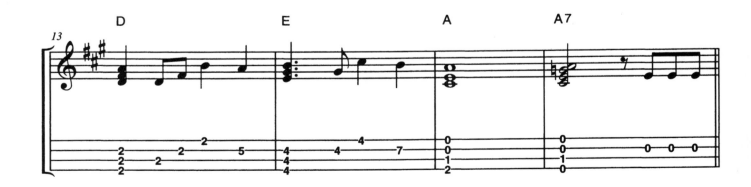

Performance Notes

"Aloha 'Oe" is one of the most popular songs of all time. It was written in 1884 by Lydia Lili'uokalani, the last Queen of Hawaii. The title translates as "Farewell to Thee."

This melody may be slightly different than the one you are familiar with – although most people now sing the first line of the chorus – "A-lo-ha 'Oe" – as a series of four ascending syllables, this arrangement is closer to the original melody.

Measure 2: Play the G♯ using your pinky while holding down the D chord – this will add a nice legato feeling to your playing.

Measure 3: The little A^{sus} arpeggio brings you back to the melody and adds some interest to what would otherwise be an entire measure filled with a single chord. You'll encounter a variation in measure 11.

If you wish, slide into the note on beat 3.

Measures 5 & 6: I've added some additional notes to the basic melody to create a sound similar to the alternating bass of Hawaiian slack key guitar. This motif crops up again and again in this arrangement.

Play the chord on beat one of measure 6 with a barre on the fourth fret. The passing chord on beat three is just to get you back down the neck.

Measures 7 & 8: If you want, throw in some light strumming to break up the 6 beats on the E7 chord. Or try adding a fingerpicked pattern of your own.

Measures 9 - 12: A slight variation of the melody from the first 4 bars. Note the way measure 9, beat 4 anticipates the next chord.

Measures 13 & 14: Play the D and E chords as full bars on the 2nd and 4th frets. Technically, these would be a D6 and an E6. Sweet, huh?

Measures 17 - 32: This is the chorus, for many people the only part of the song they have ever heard. For a real traditional sound, try to play all the chords with a nice smooth tremolo. Or add some gentle strums to fill out the measures with half and whole note chords.

Measures 21 & 22: Just to break things up a bit, I go back to slack key-style, with the addition of slides and some extra notes to simulate the alternating bass a guitarist would use.

Measures 31 & 32: If you want to keep playing, either go back to the top of the tune or just repeat the chorus with your own variations. Otherwise, ritard slightly at the A^{sus} chord.

Here are the barre chords you will use to play to "Aloha 'Oe":

On Pronouncing Hawaiian

Hawaiian is quite easy to pronounce; simply take the time to say each letter.

Vowels are similar to Spanish:

a = "ah" as in "father"
e = "eh" as in "hay"
i = "ee" as in "see"
o = "oh" as in "below"
u = "oo" as in "pool"

Vowel pairs may give you a little trouble. Again, just remember to say each letter.

"Kaulana Na Pua" sounds like "KAH - oo - la - na na poo -ah"

The consonants are also similar to Spanish, save the w, which is part way between a "w" and a "v" sound. The 'okina (') is a special case; pronounce it as a slight pause for breath, as when you say "uh-oh!"

So "E Ku'u Morning Dew" is "Ay Koo - oo Morning Dew." And "Kī Hō'alu," the Hawaiian name for slack key guitar, is "kee HOH - ah - loo."

One final note before we get started: throughout this book I use the Hawaiian spelling for the instrument: 'ukulele. The name joins two words: *lele*, which means "leap or jump," and *'uku*, or flea (well, louse, actually.) So say "oo - koo - leh - leh."

Wehiwehi 'Oe

S. Kalama

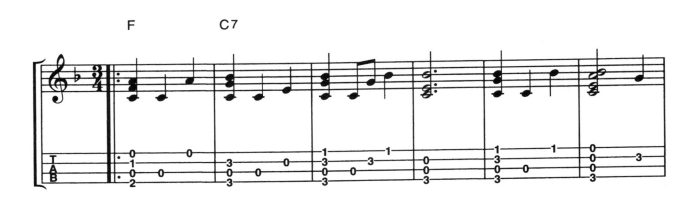

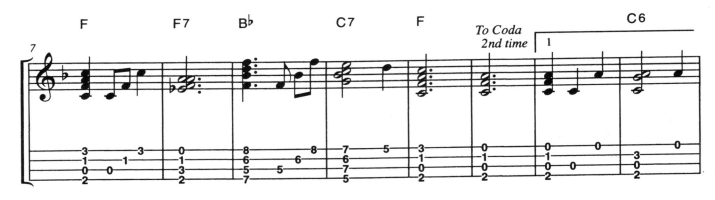

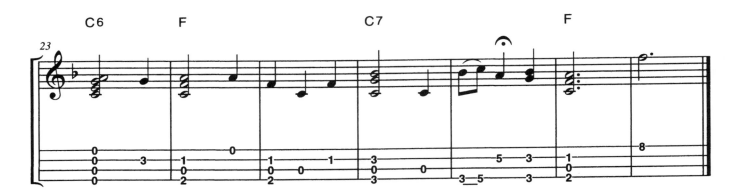

Performance Notes

"Wehiwehi 'Oe," which translates as "Thou Art Beautiful," ranks among the sweetest of the many 19th Century Hawaiian waltzes.

Using broken chords and open strings to add rhythmic interest, this arrangement may be played using any combination of your thumb and fingers. I like to roll the chords slightly by placing my thumb on the 4th string and using one finger per string – plucking them very rapidly in succession. You can get much the same effect with a slow strum.

Measure 2: This partial voicing of a C7 chord is a nice change of pace. From your F chord, simply drop your ring finger to the third fret, fourth string, and use your pinky on the third. Try to place both fingers together; then lift your pinky for beat 2. Notice that the first string is not sounded.

Measures 3 – 6: Another C7 voicing - drop the index finger down to the first fret. You'll get some practice removing and replacing your index and pinky will holding down the Bb on the fourth string.

Measures 9 & 10. Both the Bb and the C7 chords are played with a barre at the fifth fret.

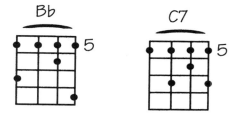

Measures 13 – 16: The first ending has you moving up both the 2nd & 4th strings before coming to rest with a G augmented triad. Hold the note under the fermata slightly longer than the time value of the chord to let the arrangement breathe.

Measure 20: Go back to the top and start over. At this point I usually vary the picking patterns slightly – adding more notes from each chord than written, or leaving some out. Rather than write out all the variations I'll leave it to you to find your own.

Measure 21: Gradually slow down as you play the coda to bring the song to a restful finish.

Measure 27: Although it isn't written, you can keep your fingers on both the 2nd & 4th strings for the slide. Little fingering tricks like this help give your playing that *nahenahe* sweetness so important to Hawaiian music.

All Through the Night

Traditional Welsh

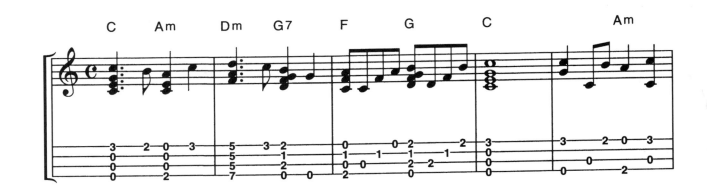

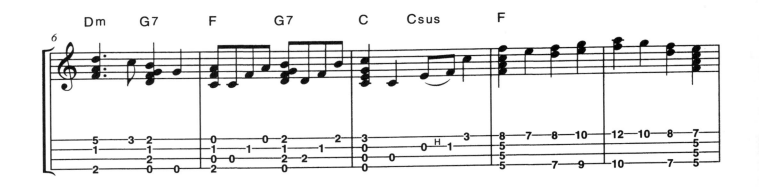

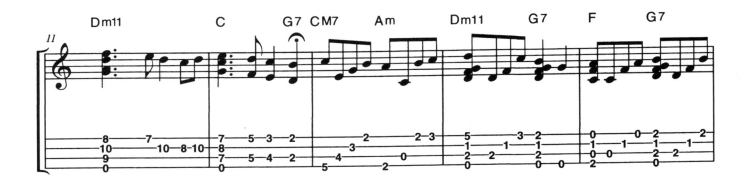

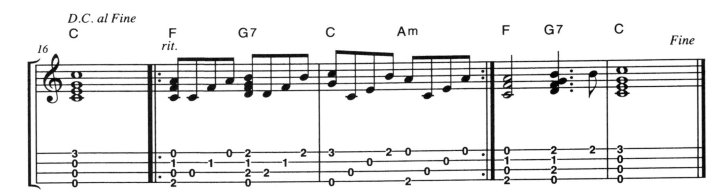

Performance Notes

Here's another look at one of songs we played earlier. This arrangement uses arpeggios and chord substitutions to lend a stately grace to this lovely lullaby. To build an even longer arrangement, play the basic version first, then add this one. That should be long enough to calm any restless baby.

No need to play it quickly, take your time and let each note ring out. I play this using my thumb and three fingers.

Measure 3: This measure adds arpeggios on the first three strings to fill out the melody. Try using one finger per string and let the notes roll off your fingers.

Measure 4: Just to break things up a bit, the picking pattern changes to a basic alternating thumb pattern on the 3rd and 4th strings.

Measure 6: The chord might be a bit of a stretch. Try not to play the open 3rd string - otherwise you'll be playing a Dm7 chord.

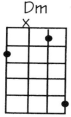

Dm

Measures 9 & 10: Play the double stops as pinches with your thumb and index finger. The sweet chord on beat 4 of measure 10 is an Fmaj7.

Measure 11: Adding the open G to a Dm triad yields this unusual chord. Another name for it would be "Dm add 4." It is simply a familiar Gm shape moved up to the 8th fret. You'll encounter another way to play this chord in a few measures.

Dm11

Measure 12. The C chord is also a familiar shape, this time a G major played at the 7th fret. Be sure to play the open G string. Let the notes under the fermata sound just a little longer than normal.

C

Measure 16: Go back to the beginning and play all the way through to the end. Gradually slow down as you repeat measures 17 & 18.

Dona Nobis Pacem

Anonymous

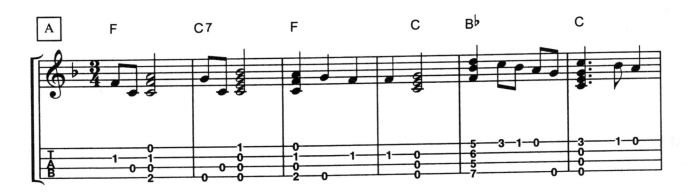

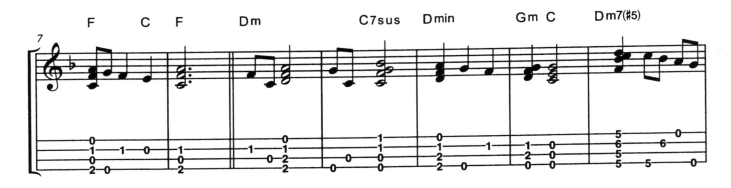

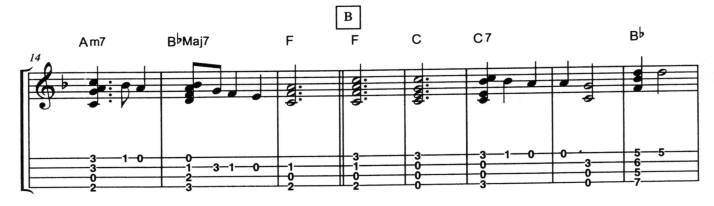

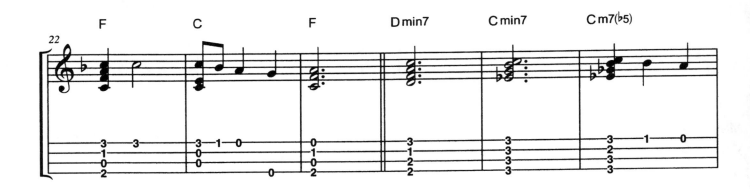

Performance Notes

A beautiful song with an enduring wish – "Give us peace" – "Dona Nobis Pacem" dates from the 16th Century. It usually takes the form of a canon, that is a round with each voice entering in sequence. Here, I have arranged it so that you play each strain twice – first with fairly simple harmony, the second time with the melody reharmonized.

Other than some of the unfamiliar chords, the arrangement is not at all challenging. Play slowly and let the chords ring out. This is a good piece to practice moving into some of the more unusual chord positions you'll encounter later in the book.

As you play through this book, you'll notice the same chord shape may have several different names. For instance, this shape is called a Asus7#5 here while in another arrangement it may be called a Dm11, or a Gadd2:

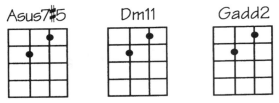

Likewise the familiar Dm7 chord shape could be called an F6, and the Am7 is also a C6:

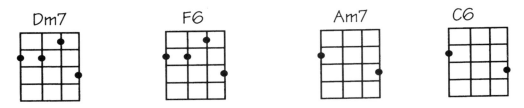

Why? The short answer is that chords are named based on where the arranger wants the harmony to move. Even though the Dm7 and F6 chords look and sound the same on your 'ukulele, a bassist would most likely play the notes D & A against a Dm7, and an F & C for the F6. Also, although the "grips" on the 'ukulele are the same, a different instrument may voice them differently.

So don't be alarmed by the odd-sounding chord names – most of the fingerings are quite easy.

Galliarde

Anonymous

Performance Notes

Here's something a little different: a Renaissance dance by the famous and prolific composer Anonymous.

Friends in the Early Music world tell me the 'ukulele is tuned the same way as the Renaissance guitar, so perhaps the inclusion of this piece isn't so farfetched after all. It is not all that difficult to play, and certainly adds a nice bit of Old World charm to your repertoire.

Track #12

The Southwind

Traditional Irish

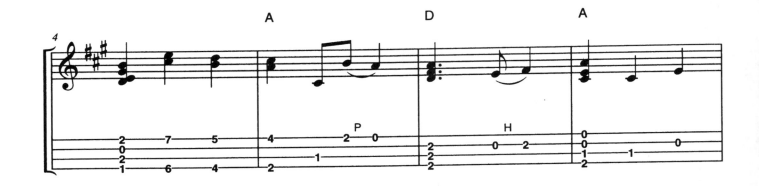

Performance Notes

"The Southwind" was introduced to North American audiences by the Irish group The Chieftains in the 1970s. It has since become a staple in the folk music world for dances, concerts and sessions.

This arrangement is fairly simple, with some slides, hammer-ons and pull-offs to liven things up a bit.

Pickup measure: Begin the tune with a quick slide from the 7th to the 5th fret. Be sure to let each note sound for its full duration.

Measure 3: If you wish, add some gentle strums on beats 2 & 3 to help the dancers find the beat.

Measure 8: Go back to the beginning of the tune and start again. The next time though, skip this measure and play the second ending (measure 9) instead.

Measures 24 & 25: The Asus chord is like a pause for breath. When you reach the end, go right back and play the whole song over again – if you were playing for a waltz, you might play it though six or seven times before the dancers were finished.

Greensleeves

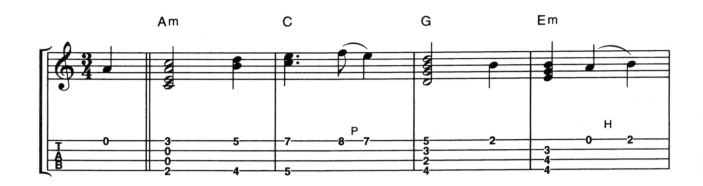

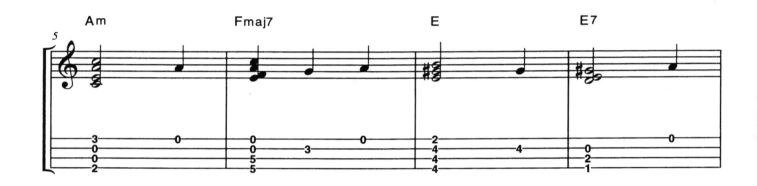

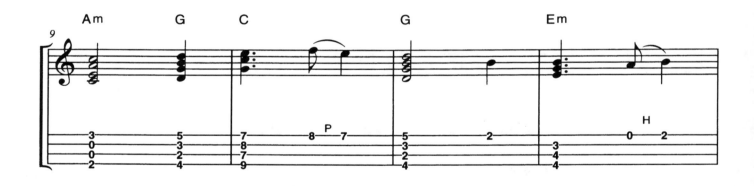

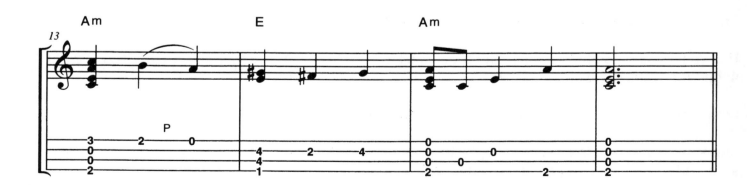

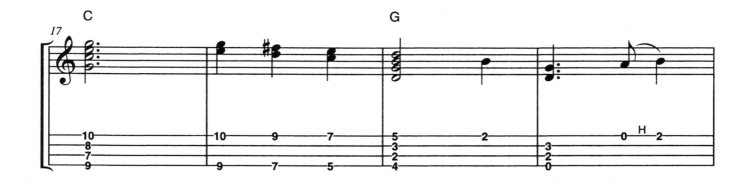

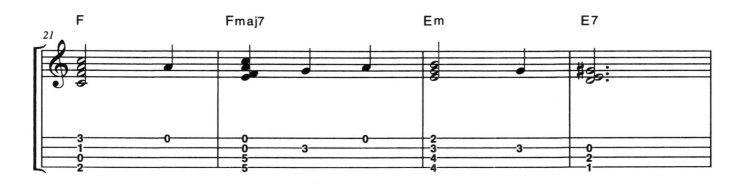

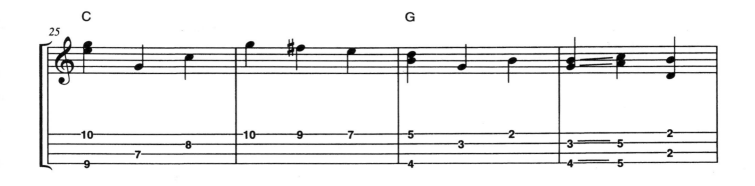

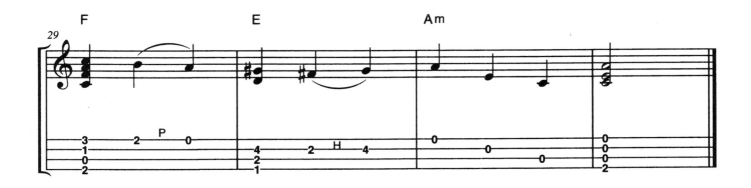

Performance Notes

First printed in 1580, "Greensleeves" has enduring charm. Many people know this melody under its Christmastime title: "What Child is This?" It has also been collected from the folk tradition in the Appalachian Mountains, where this version of the melody comes from.

The arrangement, while not too challenging, uses some unfamiliar chord shapes and double stops.

Measure 1 & 2: Play the double stops as pinches with your thumb and index finger.

Measure 3: This is simply a variation of a familiar G chord. Because the note on beat 3 is on the second fret, I play this measure while holding a barre at fret 2 and reach up to the 5th fret with my pinky:

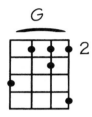

Measure 6: The $F^{maj}7$ chord is a nice change of pace and leads into the Em chord in the next measure. If you sound it using your ring finger and pinky, you can reach back with your index finger to play the note on beat 3 without losing the chord.

Measure 9 & 10: Just like the beginning, only here you play the full chords.

Measure 17 & 25: This is the same fingering as the G chord in measure 3, moved up the neck. Play it with a barre on the 7th fret.

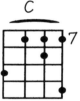

Measure 27: Though it may not be obvious from looking at the TAB, this is best played using the G chord barred at fret 2 from measure 3.

Measure 32: Many people end this song with an A major chord, rather than the A minor given here. Your choice.

Hilo March

Joseph K. 'Ae'a

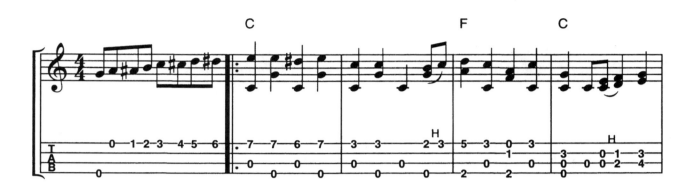

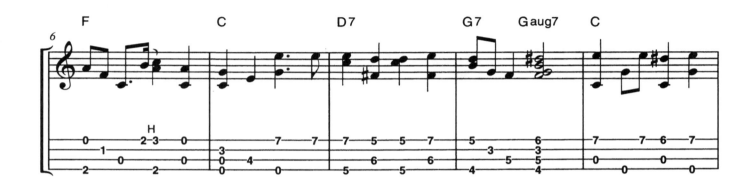

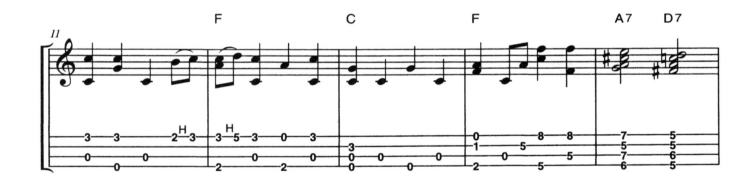

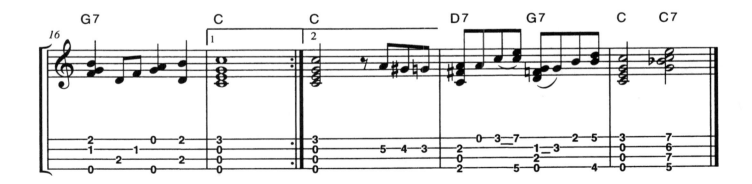

Performance Notes

"Hilo March" was a favorite of the Royal Hawaiian Band. It has found its way into the repertoire of many mainland steel guitarists and it's also the fight song of the University of Hawaii at Hilo.

This arrangement makes extensive use of a guitar technique – sometimes called "Travis Picking" or "Thumb Picking" – where the thumb keeps up a steady alternating bass on the lowest strings. Since the 'ukulele uses a reentrant tuning, with the fourth string tuned higher than it would be on a guitar, the technique can create some unusual harmonies.

Measure 1: Nothing like a little chromatic run up the fingerboard to set up the ragtime feeling of this sprightly tune. To keep the jazzy feel, try to swing the notes a bit.

Measures 2 & 3: To achieve the alternating bass effect, play the 3rd & 4th strings with your thumb and the other strings with your index and middle fingers. If this technique is new to you, make an exercise out of these two measures: play them very slowly until you can easily control your thumb.

Measure 3: Notice that the thumb pattern has switched – now you play the 4th string on beats one & three. If you can play the long stretch on beat one from a first position F6 chord, so much the better.

F6

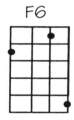

Measure 4: Break the "thumb on string 3 rule" to play the double stop after beat 2, then hammer on. It's a nice trick to move you up to the next chord.

Measures 6 & 7: Things start to get pretty syncopated here. Keep up the alternating thumb and you'll be fine.

Measure 8: Play this measure while holding a barre at the 5th fret.

D9

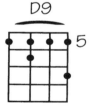

Measure 10: Just like measure 2, only a little more syncopated.

Measure 13: Take advantage of the open "C" string on beat 2 to move up to a barre at the 5th fret.

Measures 19-20: Another variation on the "Hawaiian Turnaround."

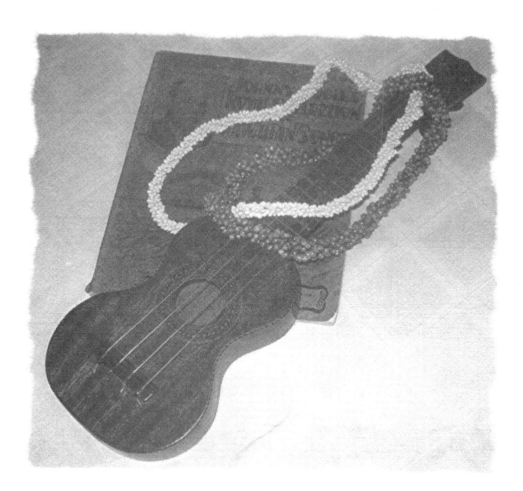

A vintage soprano 'ukulele from an unnamed maker.

New Spanish Fandango

Traditional

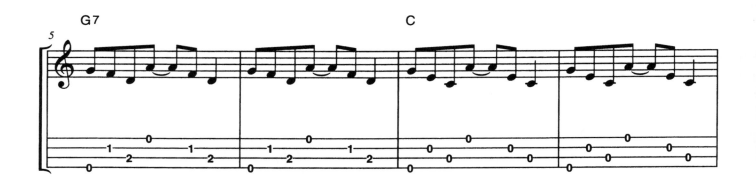

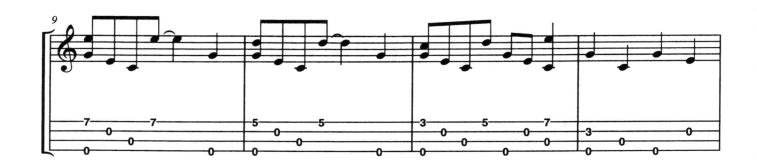

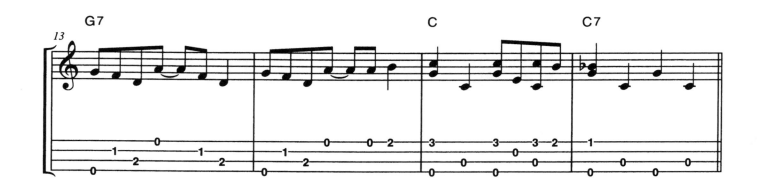

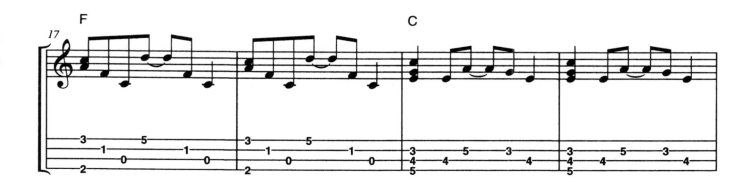

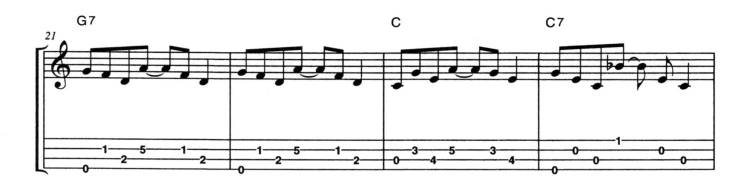

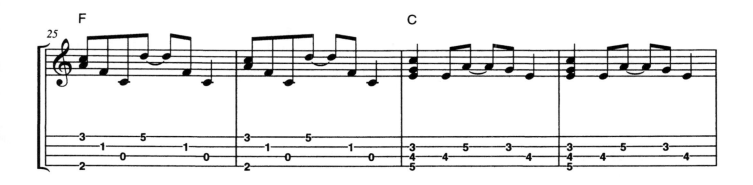

Performance Notes

Henry Worrall's Nineteenth Century parlor guitar piece "Spanish Fandango" has enjoyed tremendous popularity – it has even entered the folk idiom. To this day country blues guitarists refer to open G tuning as "Spanish" tuning because the piece was written in that tuning. I first learned it as a high school student by listening to recordings of Mississippi John Hurt, who called it "Spanish Flang Dang."

This arrangement is built upon several different folk guitar versions. Throughout the song, you'll play the 3rd and 4th strings with your thumb and use one or two fingers for the melody notes. I think the ukulele's high G string creates a nice "music box" effect when played this way.

Measure 1 - 4: If you are not used to playing alternating bass with your thumb, these 4 measures will show you how! Play the down beat of each measure as a pinch with your thumb & index finger. Try to keep the pattern smooth. Note that in measure 3 you play the melody note after beat 2 between two thumb strokes.

Measures 5-8: Continue playing strings 3 & 4 with your thumb. Notice that you don't play on beat three – this helps push the syncopation. Although technically the chords you play are a G9 and C6, an accompanist would play the G7 and C chords written above the staff.

Measures 9 & 10: This is the same picking pattern as the previous two measures.

Measures 17 & 18: Play these out of a first position F chord. Use your pinky to reach up to the 5th fret.

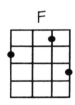

Measures 19 & 20: There are a couple of ways to play the chord on the downbeat: with a quick downward brush with your thumb; as a pinch using your thumb, index and middle fingers; or, the way I play it, as a thumb down stroke on the 4th and 3rd string followed immediately by an upward brush with the index finger. It's weird, but it works!

Measure 22: Change your picking pattern so the downbeat is played on the open C string.

E Ku'u Morning Dew

Eddie Kamae

slack key style

49

Performance Notes

Kī Hō'alu, or slack key guitar, is a fingerpicked guitar style native to Hawai'i. Utilizing lush open tunings, sweet harmonies, and a laid-back approach, it is instantly recognizable. Slack key is thought to have developed starting in the 1830s, well before the introduction of the 'ukulele, so it is only natural that many Islands musicians would adapt it to the "little guitar."

This arrangement of "E Ku'u Morning Dew" is based on the way a slack key guitarist would approach the tune. It features numerous slides, parallel sixths and thirds, and the tricky syncopation common to the style. It works equally well on instruments with a low G string – a common stringing in Hawai'i. Simply play the TAB as written - the harmonies will take care of themselves.

For a longer arrangement, combine this with the more basic version you learned earlier.

Pickup measure: Be sure to let each note of the slides ring out for its full value. Though it may not be immediately apparent from the TAB, this measure is fingered as a series of double stops on the 1st and 3rd strings.

Measure 3: Note the harmony change from the earlier arrangement. Slack key arrangements often change the chords to take advantage of open strings. Play the hammer-ons after beat three as a smooth double stop.

Measure 5: Another example of the slack key style of using double stops instead of complete chords. Be careful with the timing of the long slide.

Measure 6: The F "chord" includes a G note on the open string – yet another example of the kinds of harmony common to the style. Both the G and F chord fragments are played using similar fingerings:

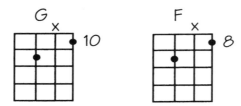

Measure 10: Play the hammer-on as a very quick grace note. Notice that you suggest the chord change without playing the F chord.

Measure 15: Hammer-on to the tonic just ahead of the downbeat in the following measure.

Measure 17: The second ending acts as a coda. Slow down gradually as you repeat the last phrase of the song and then play a typical Hawaiian turnaround to bring the song to a restful conclusion.

Once you've mastered playing this arrangement, you might want to try some of these techniques on some other songs.

A lei of 'ukulele. Left to right: Po Mahina tenor, Kei Lani six-string tenor, vintage soprano (builder unknown), Wood Magic concert, Hilo concert.

Over the Rainbow

E.Y. Harburg/Harold Arlen

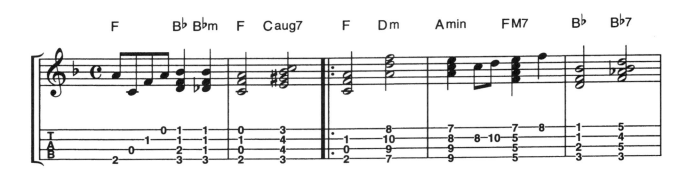

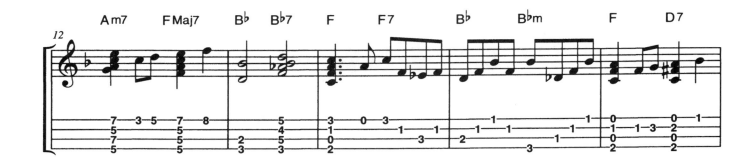

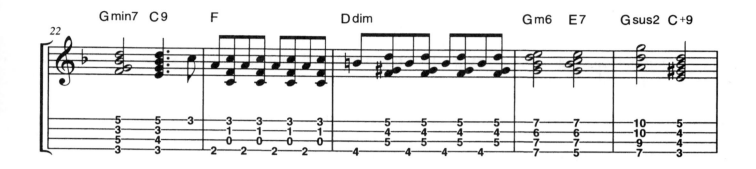

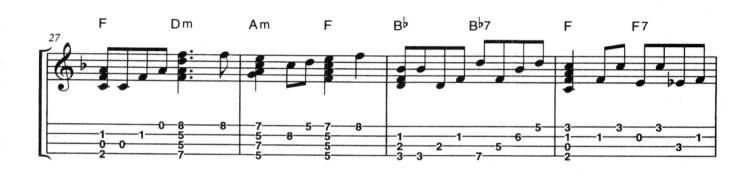

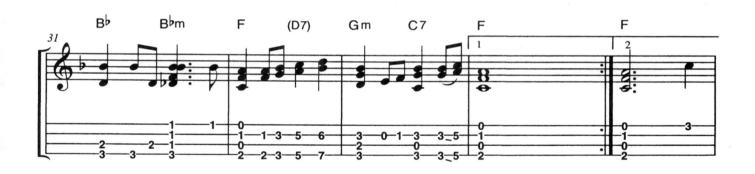

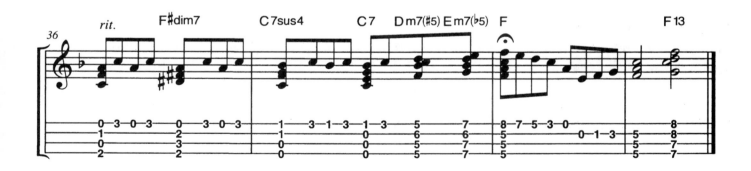

Performance Notes

Some great songs never go out of style. "Yip" Harburg and Harold Arlen's immortal "Over the Rainbow" first appeared in the musical "The Wizard of Oz," now a whole new generation has fallen in love with it again thanks to Israel Kamakawiwo'ole's hauntingly beautiful singing and 'ukulele playing.

This arrangement sticks close to the original melody and chord changes. It uses some jazz chords and arpeggios, but really isn't too difficult.

Measures 1 & 2: Play the introduction rubato, that is, without any strict tempo.

Measure 3: It may be easier to play the Dm chord using a barre at the 7th fret:

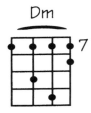

Measure 11: The 8 bar melody repeats itself starting here. "Over the Rainbow" follows what's called the "American Popular Song Form" – two 8 measure strains that repeat in the pattern A-A-B-A. In the next 8 bars I added some slightly different chord voicings, as well as some arpeggios and runs to fill out the arrangement. Naturally, you could simply repeat measures 2-10 and then skip ahead to the B section starting at measure 20, but where's the fun in that?

Measures 21 & 22: Some fun with close harmony chord voicings to cycle back to the F chord:

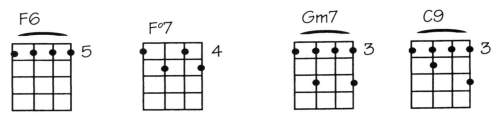

Measure 23: Playing the chord on the offbeat adds some unexpected syncopation.

Measures 25 & 26: More oddball chords. You'll encounter at least one of these voicings again with a different name later.

Measure 27: You are back at the top of the A section. After you play this section, go back to the top of the tune and play it again. Try to mix and match some of the chords and arpeggios you've learned, or make up your own.

Measures 36 - 39: Slow down and play this more like you did at the introduction. Hold the F chord on the downbeat of measure 38 for the space of a breath, then play the run in one fluid motion.

Ahi Wela

Lizzie Doirin & Mary Beckley

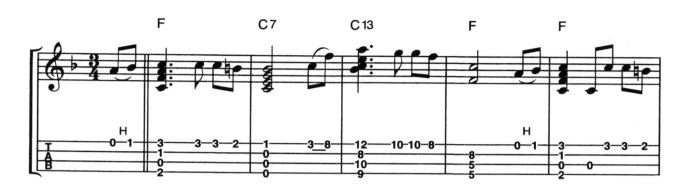

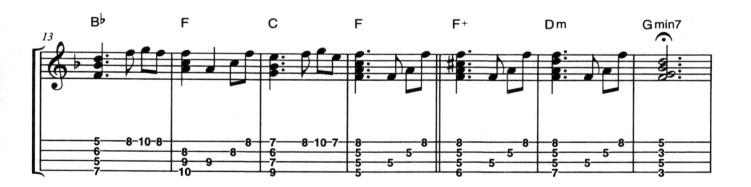

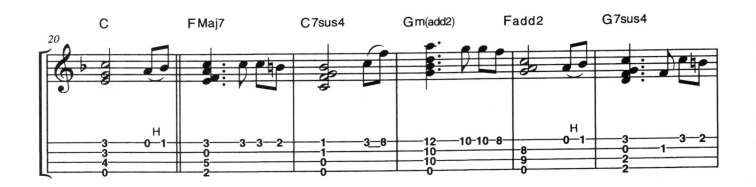

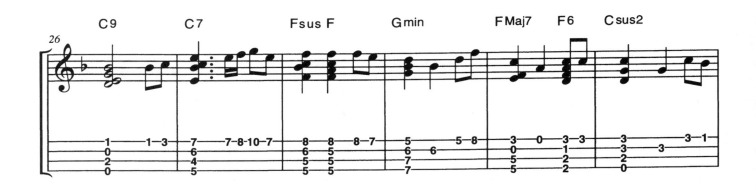

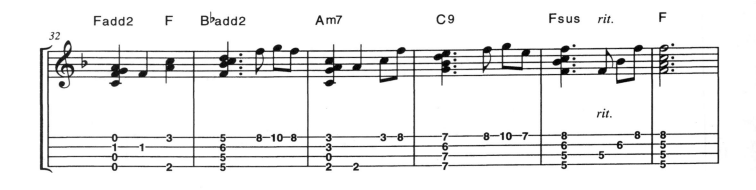

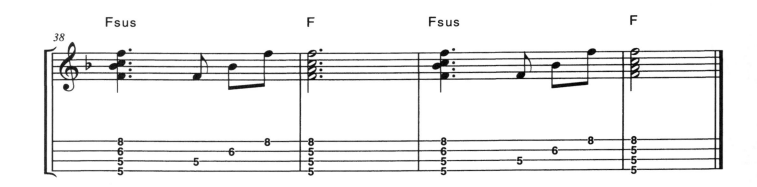

Performance Notes

"Ahi Wela" (Hot Fire) speaks eloquently of the burning passion experienced by those in love – yet it is sung and danced today by elementary-aged children all through Hawai'i! It was written in 1891 by Lizzie Doiron, a singer with the Royal Hawaiian Band, and Mary Beckley, a lady-in-waiting to Queen Lili'uokalani.

This arrangement plays through this lovely waltz twice; the first time using (mostly) familiar chords and then again slightly reharmonized to bring out the mystery of the melody.

It sounds best when you lightly roll the chords to separate the individual notes. You can accomplish this with a slow downward strum, or by using your thumb and three fingers to grab the chord and rapidly plucking each note starting with the thumb.

Measure 3: Don't be put off by the C13 chord, it's simply a C7 with the addition of an A on top. It's built from a familiar C7 voicing at the 8th fret:

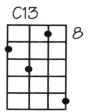

Measure 9: This measure starts the second, more familiar strain of the melody. You'll play much of this section using barre chords, such as the Bb here.

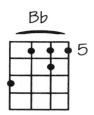

Measure 16: This is the end of the song; from here it goes into a four bar bridge and then begins again using some more challenging chords.

Measures 17 - 20: The bridge uses common tones against a chromatic run to create tension to move the arrangement back to the beginning of the song. Hold the Gm7 chord under the fermata slightly longer than it's written to let the music catch its breath.

Measure 21: We're back at the top of the melody. From here on most of the harmony uses extensions to the basic chords or substitutions. Nothing requires too great a stretch. Note that many of these same chord shapes have different names depending on how they are used. Take your time as you play. Since the melody should be familiar by now you can concentrate on the new fingerings.

Measure 36. Start to slow down as you play to the end.

Minuet in G

attributed to J. S. Bach

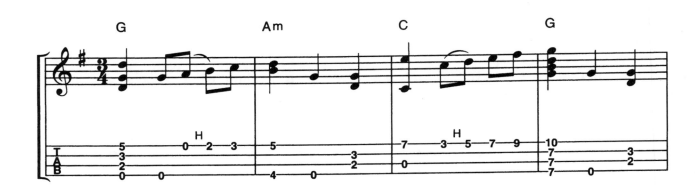

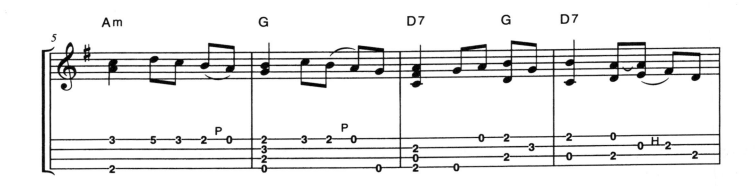

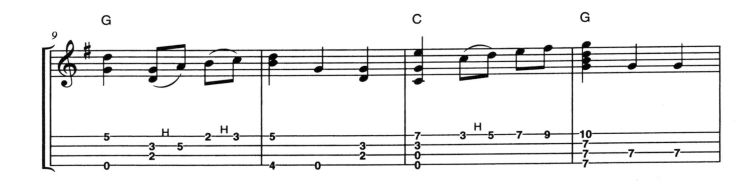

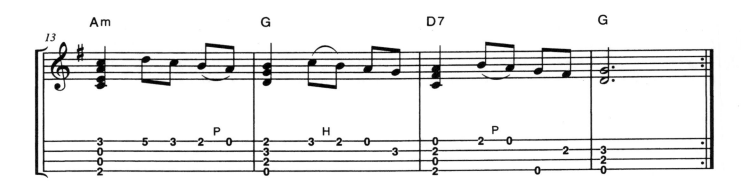

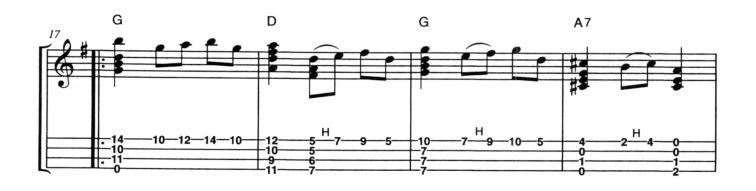

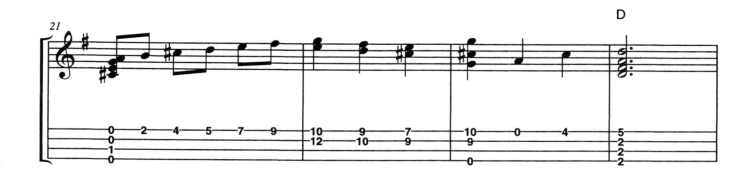

Performance Notes

This charming piece of music comes from what may be one of the most famous birthday presents ever: "The Notebook for Anna Magdelena Bach," which the composer J.S. Bach gave to his second wife in 1775. The book contains study pieces written by family members and friends, apparently copied by Bach's wife and children.

This particular piece has served as the basis for quite a number of settings, including a pop song, several movie scores, and some inspired jazz arranging. It's only fitting that we add it to the 'ukulele repertoire. I have taken a few liberties with the harmony in order to fit the arrangement easily on the fingerboard using familiar chord voicings.

Measure 1: The Notebook has this, and all subsequent eighth note passages, played legato, that is, in a smoothly flowing way. I've indicated one way to do this using hammer-ons and pull-offs. Feel free to finger these whichever way works best for you.

Measures 7 & 8: I've substituted a little internal turnaround for the bass run usually played by beginning piano students.

Measures 9 - 12: Just another way to play the first 4 bars.

Measure 18. Play the first D chord with a barre on the 9th fret:

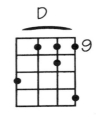

Measure: 22: Some double stops to remind us of the Latin origins of the 'ukulele.

Measure 28: Although this could be easily fingered out of a basic D chord position, I like the sound of the ringing open strings.

Measure 29: Try to play all of the hammer-ons smoothly. If you have trouble with this, simply pick each note and strive for a smooth flow.

The Ragged Little Flea

Mark L. Nelson

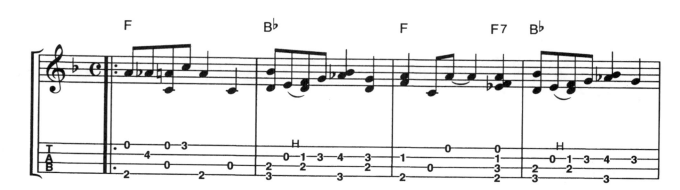

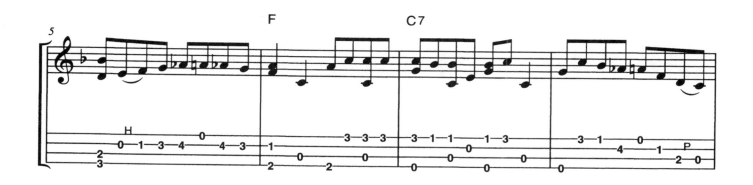

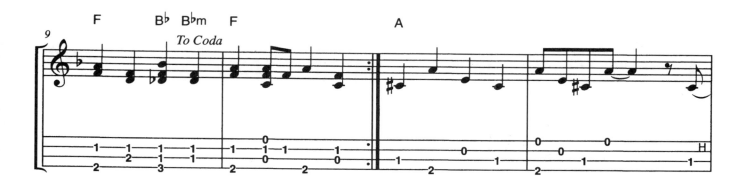

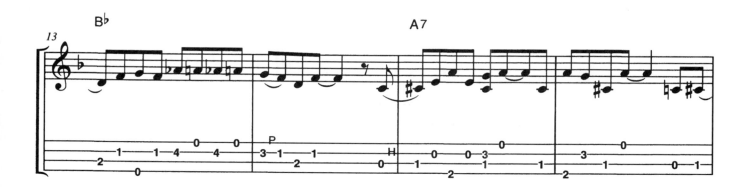

62

Performance Notes

I wrote "The Ragged Little Flea" the day I finished restoring a lovely old banjo-uke I'd rescued. It seemed to me the newly alive instrument – which was destined to be a birthday present for an old friend – needed a new song to break it in properly. And there's something about a banjo-uke that just says, "ragtime!"

The tune is based on the same kind of country blues fingerpicking as "New Spanish Fandango," although the double thumb bass isn't quite so steady as on that arrangement. Generally speaking, all of the notes on the 3rd & 4th strings are played with your thumb. Try to keep a smooth flow going, and don't forget to swing those eighth notes!

This particular arrangement sounds even better if your instrument has a low G. Just play it as written – all of the notes on the 4th string will sound an octave lower.

Measure 1: Though it doesn't look like it from the tab, I play this out of a first position F chord. Use your pinky to play both the Ab on the 2nd string and the C on the 1st string.

Measure 2 & 4: Same basic idea – play this from a Bb chord position and reach up with your pinky.

Measure 10: That's right, it's a ten bar blues form! You'll get a chance to play the more common 12 bar form in "Blue 'Ukulele Blues."

Measures 12 & 13: Pick the last note of measure 12 with your thumb and hammer on to the down beat of measure 13 to make the syncopation ring out. You'll be doing variations of this move throughout this section.

Measure 17: Notice that both beats 1 & 2 feature a double stop where one note is hammered and the other is picked with your thumb.

Measure 18: It may take a bit of practice to jump from the single notes of the previous measure up to the double stops. Play the down beat as a pinch with your thumb and index finger and quickly slide back down. Make sure each note of the slide rings out and is held for the full eighth note.

Measure 22: Go back to the top of the tune and play it again. When you get to measure 9 after the repeat, jump to the coda beginning at measure 23.

Measure 24: Play this from a G7 chord position:

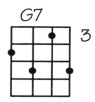

Measure 25: Play the first chord staccato; that is with a sharp attack and no sustain.

Kaulana Na Pua

Ellen Prendergast

Track #21

Performance Notes

Written by Ellen Wright Prendergast in 1893, "Kaulana Na Pua" ("Famous Are the Flowers") expresses outrage and opposition to the illegal annexation of Hawai'i by the United States. The song declares support to Queen Lili'uokalani and says that rather than accept money to sign the "paper of the enemy" the people would be content to eat "the stones of the land."

It is a remarkably beautiful and powerful song – play this arrangement with a stately grace.

Measures 1- 4: A simple picking pattern sets up a motif using suspended chords that will repeat throughout the arrangement.

Measure 11: Play the triplet with a quick flick of your finger.

Measures 18 & 19: A variation of the opening riff. After playing measure 18, go back to the sign at measure 5 and play through to the end.

Measures 25 - 28: Gradually slow down as you come to the end of the music.

Planxty Irwin

Track #22

Turlough O'Carolan

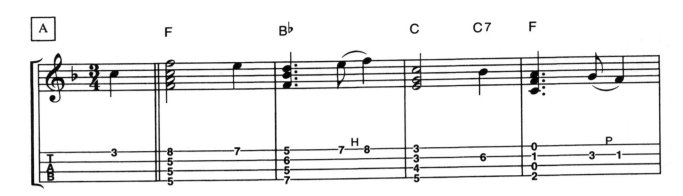

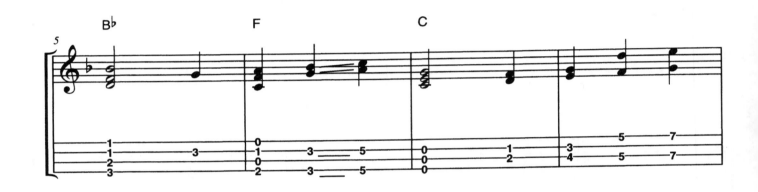

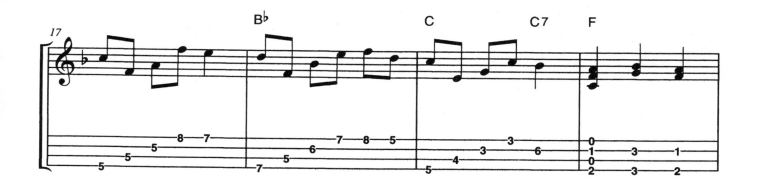

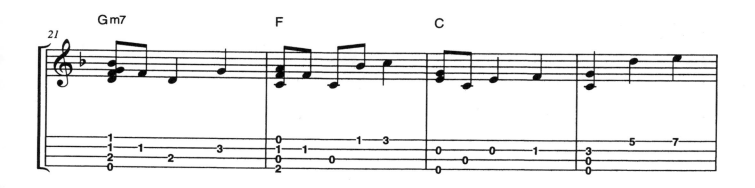

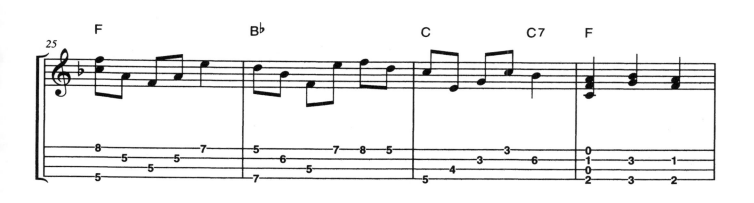

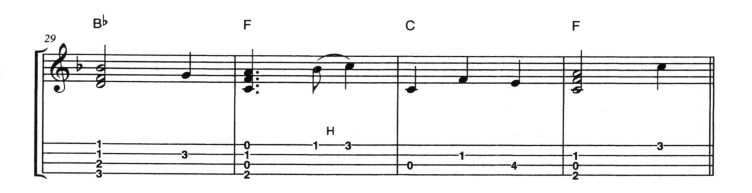

67

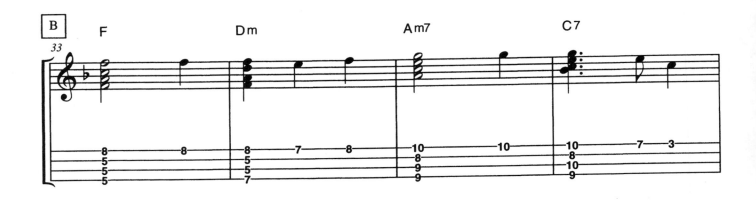

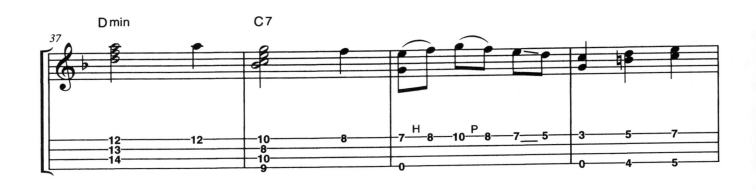

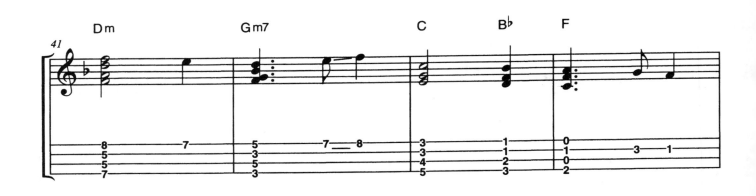

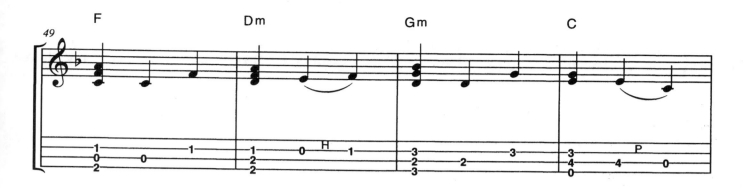

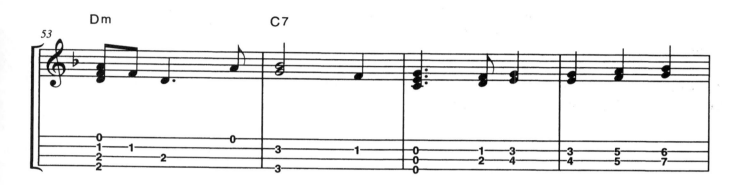

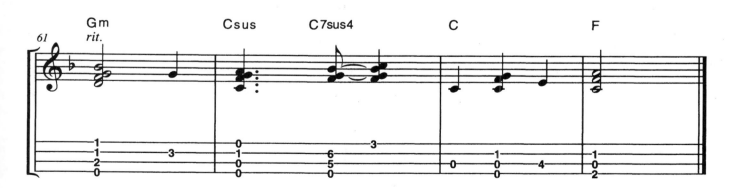

Performance Notes

The celebrated blind Irish harper Turlough O'Carolan (1670 - 1738) coined the word "planxty" for songs he wrote in honor of his many patrons. "Planxty Irwin" was written for Colonel John Irwin of County Sligo.

Irish music, like most Celtic and European folk tunes, often follows a set pattern: two strains, each repeated twice. I have written it as a waltz rather than the more common practice of notating it in 6/8 time, as I feel the tune lends itself wonderfully to dancing.

The arrangement makes extensive use of barre chords up and down the neck. Play the chords on the downbeat with a quick, rolling arpeggio, either by plucking with your thumb and three fingers or by using a down strum. Try to play it at a brisk pace and imagine a roomful of elegant dancers.

Measures 1-16: This is the first strain of the melody. Try to keep a flowing rhythm between the chords, single notes and double stops. Be sure your hammer-ons, pull-offs and slides sound each note for the full time value.

Measure 17: Rather than simply repeating the first section, I chose to fill out the melody with picked arpeggios. For the most part, the chords are exactly the same as in the first section.

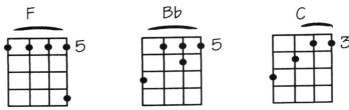

Measure 21: The Gm7 chord is quite close to a Bb – it adds a hint of Celtic melancholy that foreshadows some of the harmonies to come.

Measures 25 - 28: These are played exactly the same as Measures 17 - 20, save for the pinch on beat 1.

Measure 39: Begin with your index finger on fret 7 and hammer on with the middle finger. That leaves your pinky to play fret 10 and pull off back to 8. Finally, slide your index finger down to fret 5. Try to play the whole run as one smooth phrase.

Measure 41: Here's the same melody from the A section, reharmonized.

Measure 49: Here's the B melody played an octave lower and with a slightly different harmony.

Measure 52: Pulling off from the 4th fret takes a little getting used to. Try to get a clean sound on the open string.

Measure 62: Grab the entire C7sus4 chord in one motion so it sustains through the end of the measure.

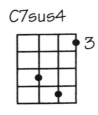

Po Mahina koa tenor 'ukulele.

Danny Boy

Traditional Irish

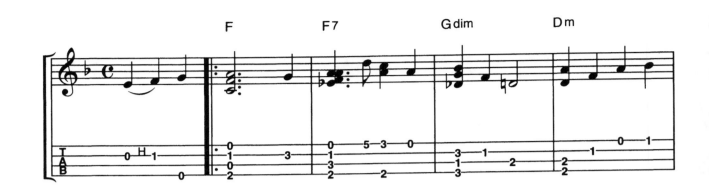

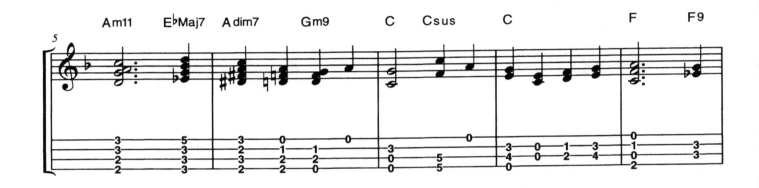

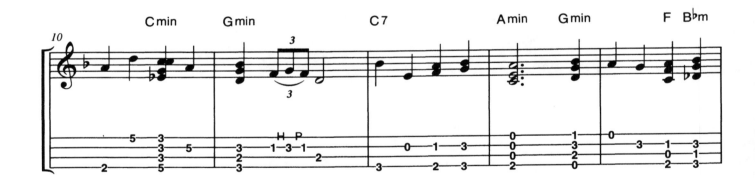

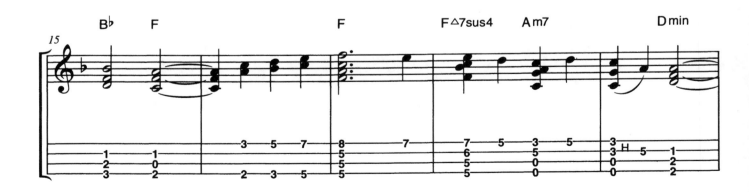

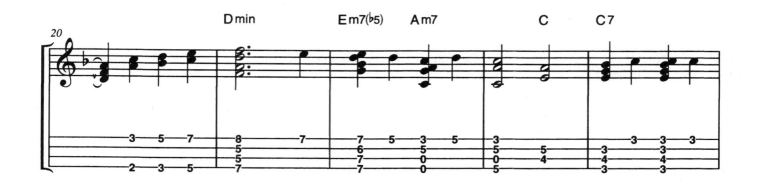

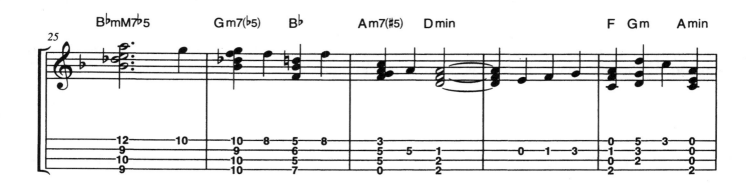

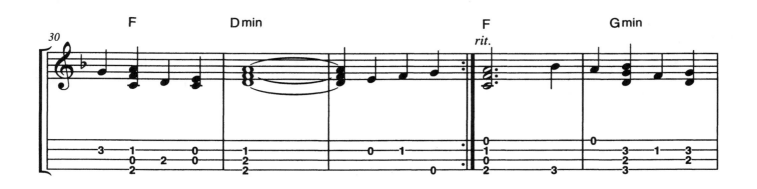

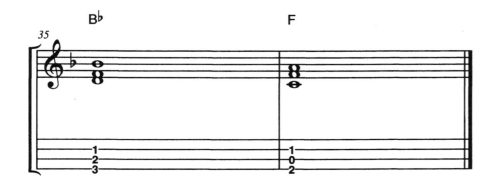

Performance Notes

Set to the traditional Irish "Londonderry Air," "Danny Boy" has become one of the best-known songs of all time. It has been used as a TV theme song, arranged for western swing square dances, inspired countless parodies, and even entered the radio mainstream a couple of times.

This arrangement stays close to the haunting melody, but uses some jazz-style chord substitutions. Play it with a strong swing feel, and feel free to embellish as much as you want.

Measure 2: The chord on the downbeat could just as easily be called a Bbm. (See measure 14). By naming it a Gdim, it sets up a nice pattern in the bass for another musician to follow, as well as lends itself to some interesting possibilities for improvising. As you play through this arrangement, be aware that many of the chord shapes can take on multiple roles.

Measures 5 & 6: Here's a typical chord melody style approach using a new chord for each melody note.

Measures: 6 & 7: The suspended lick that starts on beat 3 and ends on the downbeat of measure 7 echoes the melody from the two previous measures. Play it softly, than increase your volume again for the ascending double stops that lead you back into the melody.

Measure 11: I couldn't resist throwing in a little Celtic-style triplet turn. Try to hold the fingering for the Gm chord as you play this.

Measure 15: The melody here would normally go directly to the F chord – adding the Bb for the first two beats delays the inevitable, so to speak.

Measure 16: "Danny Boy" has the same A-A-B-B structure as the other Celtic tunes in this book. This is the beginning of the B part. Typically, the B strain takes the melody higher than the A strain, one of the reasons there are so many great Irish tenors!

Measure 25. Play this wacko chord while holding a barre at the 9th fret. That's not a typo, it really is a Bb diminished triad with a major seventh on top.

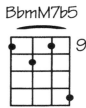

Measure 32: Go back to the top and play it all again. This time, try to vary the melody or the chords.

Measures 33 - 36: Gradually slow down as you play the coda.

Blue 'Ukulele Blues

Mark L. Nelson

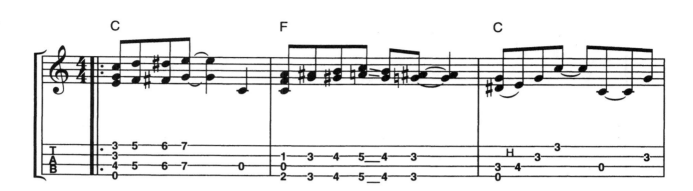

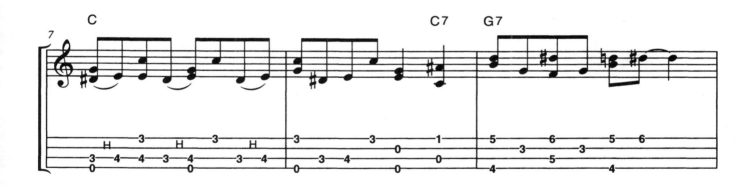

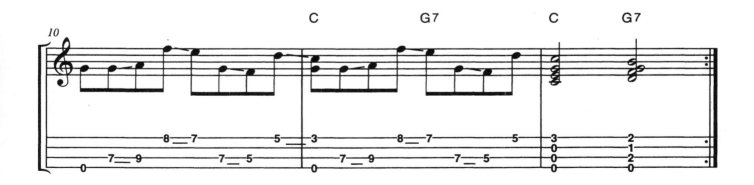

solo

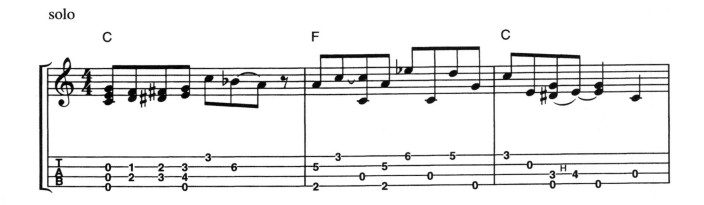

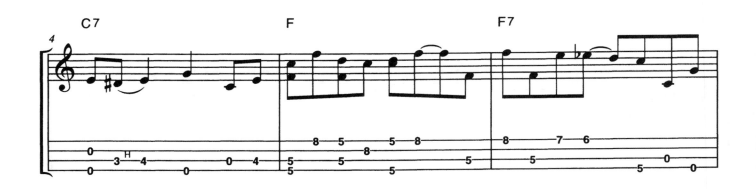

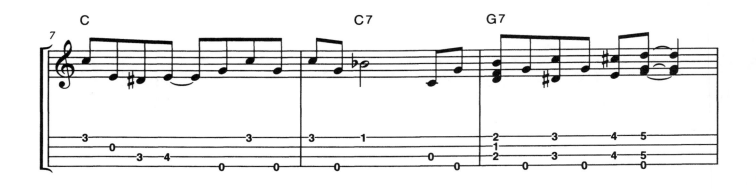

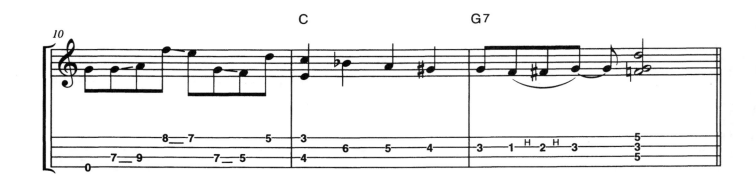

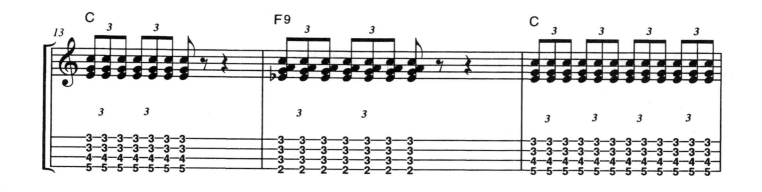

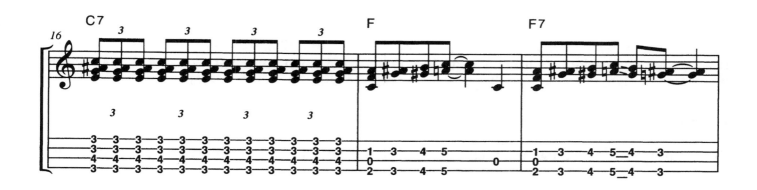

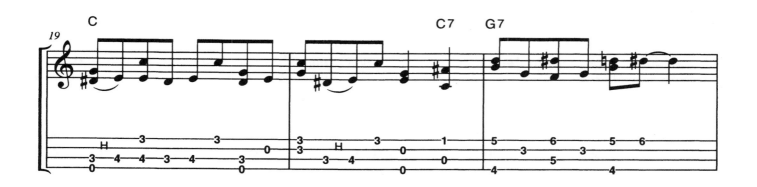

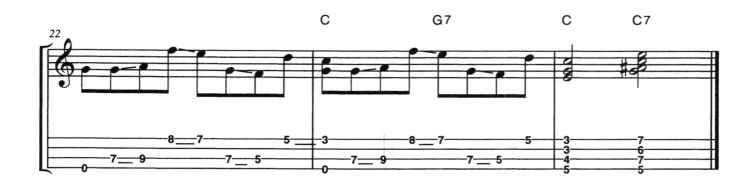

Performance Notes

I wrote "Blue 'Ukulele Blues" as an exercise to teach my students how to improvise. The song uses the 12 bar blues form, a basic building block of rock, jazz and blues and the template for literally hundreds of songs. I usually play it on an instrument with a low G; I've written it here for a standard 'ukulele tuning. It sounds just fine played either way.

Measure 1: Play the downbeat as a thumb and three finger pinch, then play the double stops with your thumb and index finger. The open string on beat four is sounded with your thumb.

Measure 3: Hold a partial barre across the first 3 strings at fret 3 and play the double stop on beat 1 with your thumb and index finger. Then move the barre down to strings 1 & 2 in time to play the open C string with your thumb on the afterbeat of beat 3.

Measure 7: The best way to approach this is to use the alternating thumb technique. So beat one is a thumb/index finger pinch. Hammer-on for the up beat, then play beat two with your thumb and middle finger. Reach up to the 3rd string with your index finger to play the upbeat. Hammer on to beat three while you pluck the 4th string with your finger, followed by another upbeat played with your middle finger. Beat four is played with your thumb again.

The pattern is continued into the next measure. Notice how this creates a "three against four" feel - be sure to add some swing to make the accents fall properly!

Measure 9: Play this out of a G7 chord – reach up to the 6th fret with your pinky.

Measures 10 & 11: If you think this sounds like a couple of classic Hawaiian turnarounds, you're right!

After measure 12, go back to the top of tune and play it again. Normally this would be where every one in the band would take a solo – if you want to try one, have a friend strum the chords while you wail away. Use the licks and runs here as your starting point and pay special attention to the blue notes.

I've included a typical solo for you to try. Notice how I've taken some of the licks from the melody and transformed them slightly. When you improvise a solo, it's a good idea to give your listeners something to hold on to.

After you've soloed to your heart's content, skip over to the next section.

Measures 13 - 16: Play the chords with a rapid up and down strum in triplet rhythm.

Wimoweh

Words and music by Solomon Linda.
Additional words and music by Ronnie Gilbert,
Lee Hays, Fred Hellerman and Pete Seeger.

Track #25

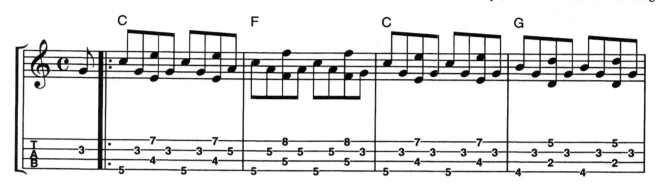

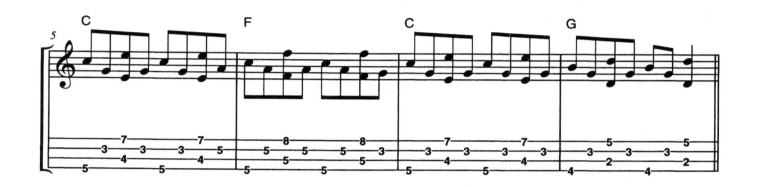

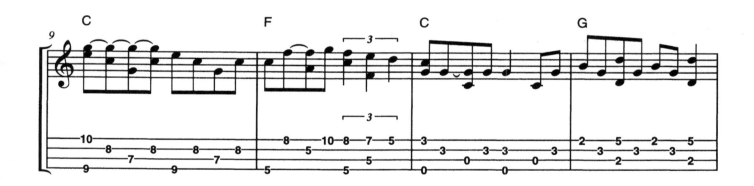

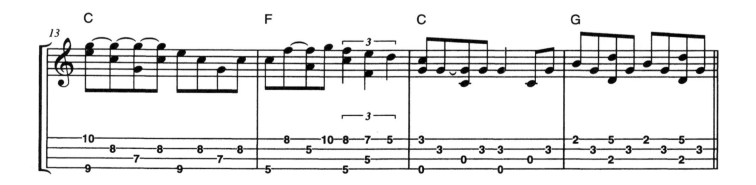

repeat and fade

Performance Notes

Few songs have had as much impact – or as odd a life – as Solomon Linda's immortal "Mbube" (pronounced "em-boo-beh"). Originally recorded on an obscure South African record label in 1939, the song captured the attention of the public and sold hundreds of thousands of copies. Years later, American folk musician Pete Seegar arranged the song for his group The Weavers, changing the name to "Wimoweh" – his misinterpretation of the Zulu words. The song became a number one hit in America – as it has done several times since.

This arrangement relies on the original recording, but takes some liberties with the order of the parts. It consists of three 8 bar sections – feel free to mix them up any order.

Measures 1-8: Play these using barre chords and reach up to the highest fret with your pinky. You will have to get in the habit of changing chords ahead of the downbeat. I use an alternating thumb pattern on strings 3 & 4.

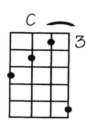 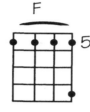 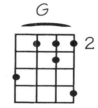

Measures 9 & 13: Hold down a barre at fret 7.

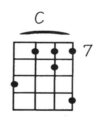

Measures 10 & 14: Play this from an F chord barred at fret 5.

Measure 17: Watch the syncopation as you play through this section. Use the picking pattern from the first 8 bars as a guide.

Measure 21: Play this using the C chord barred at the 7th fret.

Measure 24: From here, go back to the beginning and start over.

Measure 25 - 28: Repeat as many times as you want, gradually getting quieter and quieter until you put the jungle cat to bed.

Isa Lei

Traditional Fijian

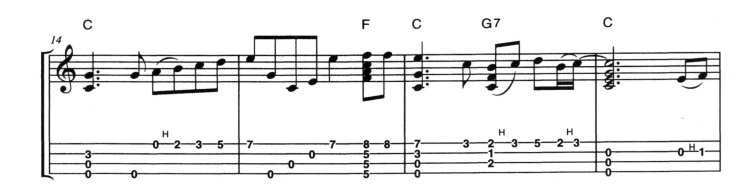

Performance Notes

Here's another look at a "Isa Lei." It starts out exactly the same as the basic arrangement, but quickly adds some twists and turns all its own, incorporating some syncopation, slides and rapid hammer-ons typical of the slack key style.

Play it with a languid, tropical feel. Use any combination of picking and strumming that's comfortable.

Measure 4: This is the first ending, go back to the beginning and play through to the second ending at measure 5. After this, things start to get a little hairy.

Measure 14: Now that we've played all the way through the song, let's add some more excitement to the melody.

Measure 16: Notice how you hammer on to the tonic just ahead of the downbeat in the next measure. Be sure to let the note sustain as you sound the chord immediately following it.

Measures 18 & 19: Parallel sixths and slides are very common to Island musical styles. Play the double stops as pinches with your thumb and index finger.

Measure 20: The C chord on beat 1 is fingered exactly like the G on beat 3, which makes it fairly easy to get all the way back down the neck in the space of a single eighth note.

 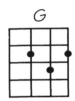

Measure 24: Another slippery little Island lick. Move your index finger down to the 1st fret for the hammer-on, then reach up to the 3rd fret with your ring finger and quickly slide it to the 5th. Playing the final note at fret 3 with your index finger sets you up for the chord on the downbeat of the next measure.

Measure 26: More fun. Use your ring finger and pinky for the hammers so you can maintain the F chord throughout this measure.

Measure 28: Slide into the double stop so you land on it right at the downbeat.

Measure 33: Play the harmonics by lightly touching the strings at the 12th fret.

Gaviotas

Mark L. Nelson

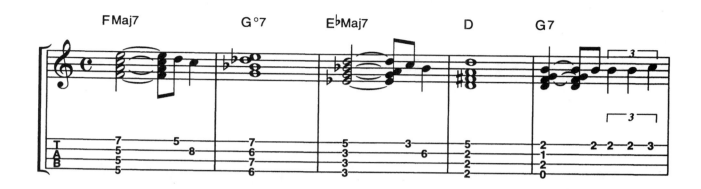

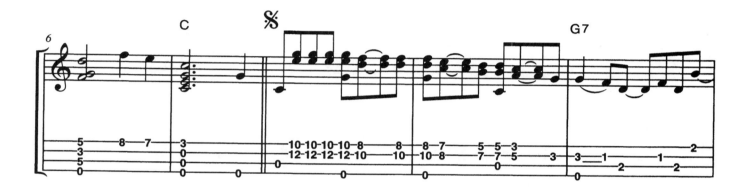

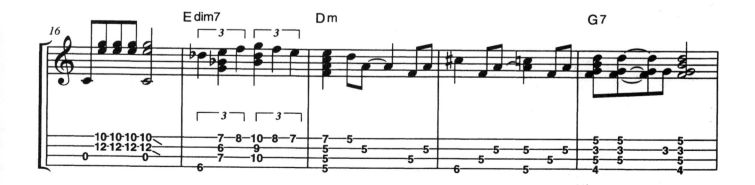

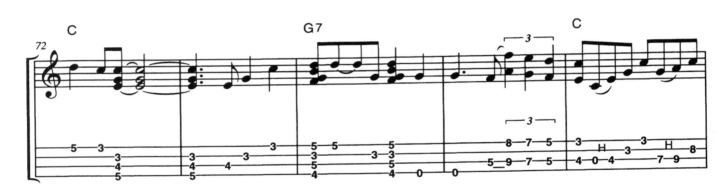

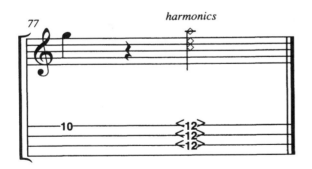

Performance Notes

The final arrangement in the book brings it all together: unusual chords up and down the neck, parallel thirds, slides, hammer-ons and pull-offs, strums and alternating thumb picking. It is quite a challenge, but well worth it for the workout it will give you.

"Gaviotas" (Spanish for sea gull) is a celebration for a beautiful stretch of the Central California coastline. I originally wrote it on the guitar and its heritage is readily apparent in the way you have to use your thumb and fingers. However, I much prefer to play it on the 'ukulele and I hope you like it, too. It works equally well on an instrument with a low G – simply play the TAB as written.

Measures 1- 7: Play the introduction freely, with no strict tempo. Roll the chords as a quick arpeggio with your thumb and three fingers. Watch the timing of the triplets in measure 5 – a motif you'll meet again and again.

Measures 8 & 9: The descending parallel thirds figure features some tricky syncopation. Be careful how you play the open strings with your thumb.

Measures 10 &11: Slide down into a basic G7 chord to play these two measures.

Measure 13: Quickly slide into the seventh fret from somewhere lower on the neck.

Measure 16: Play the double stop at beat 3, then slide it down to a lower position just before the next downbeat. It doesn't really matter how far you slide, the idea is just to have the notes fall as they fade.

Measure 33: Play the chord as a quick down strum with a sharp attack and immediately mute it by slightly lifting all of your fingers slightly off of the fingerboard.

Measure 42: Let the initial note ring for its full value before you play the slide. By now you should be fairly familiar with double stops like these.

Measure 44: This is essentially just a picking pattern to fill out the G7 chord. Feel free to substitute your own pattern in this and other similar measures.

Measures 52 & 53: Finger these as a series of descending double stops on the 1st & 3rd strings.

Measure 56: This starts a long bridge section that's similar to the intro. Either roll or strum the initial chord. For the most part this section uses an alternating thumb technique on the 3rd & 4th strings. Look to the TAB to see how to finger each chord.

Measure 62 & 63: Play this while holding down an Fm chord:

Fm

Measure 70: Go back to the sign at measure 8 and play down to measure 31. At measure 31, jump to the coda beginning at measure 71.

Measure 77 & 78: Play the ascending licks using chord inversions rather than fingering individual notes to create a legato feel. The first is simply a C chord. I play the lick starting after beat 2 with a partial bar at the 7th fret, ending up with this chord shape:

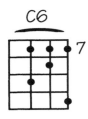

Finally, play the harmonics by lightly holding your finger directly above the 12th fret. Move your picking hand back towards the bridge slightly to make the notes ring out.

Chord Inversions

Hilo concert 'ukulele handpainted by Leilehua Yuen.

Chord Inversions

major triads

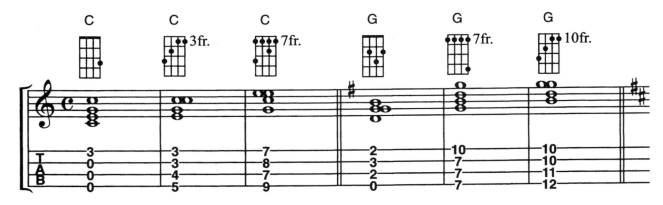

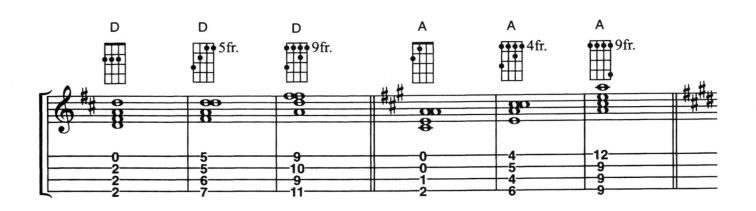

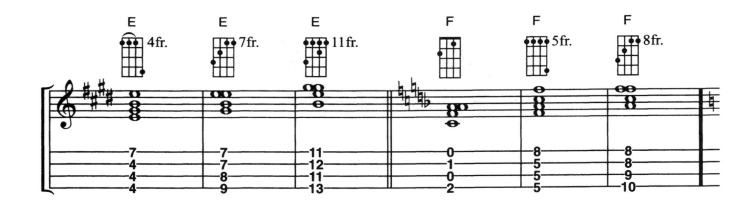

92

dominant 7ths

93

minor triads

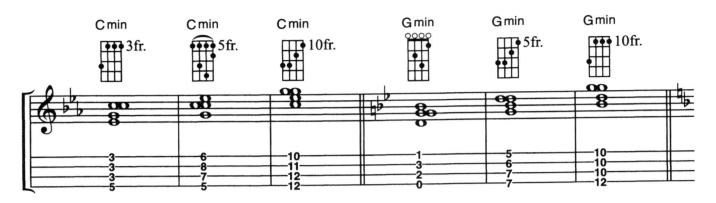

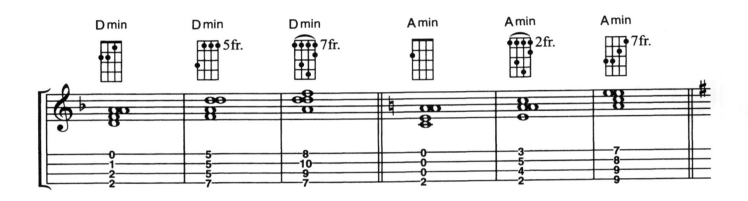

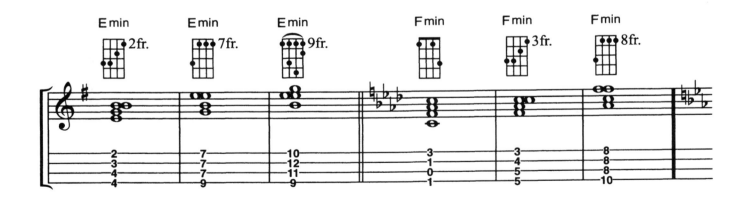

minor 7th

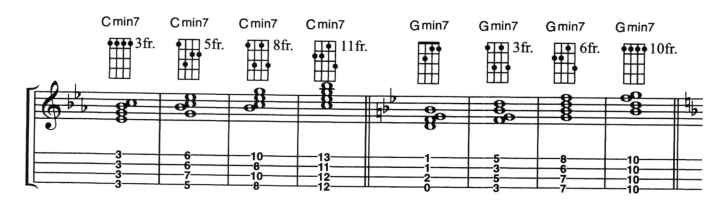

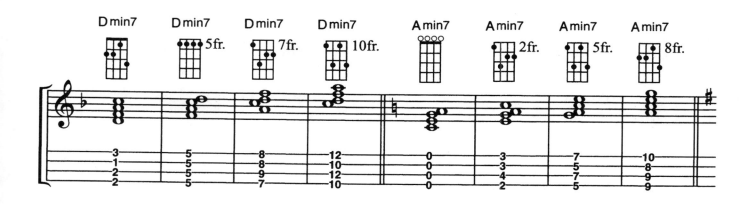

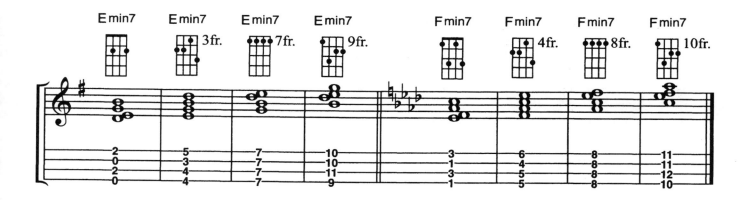

Mark Nelson

photo – Helga Motley

Multi-instrumentalist Mark Nelson has carved a unique niche for himself as an entertainer, musician and educator. His deep love and understanding of traditional music led him to the mastery of several different musical idioms, ranging from old time western music to Celtic to Hawaiian. In a career that began well before he was able to drive, he has performed everywhere from street corners to festivals and the concert stage in the US, Europe and Canada. He once worked as a banjo playing gorilla in Dublin, but that's a different story.

Mark's mastery of the Appalachian dulcimer won him a first place in the National Dulcimer Championships in 1979. Lately it is his guitar and 'ukulele playing that is getting the most notice, making him an in-demand instructor at camps and festivals across the US. He has appeared at such prestigious venues as "A Prairie Home Companion," the Letterkenny, Ireland International Folk Festival, and the halftime show for the Skagway, Alaska, Girls Junior Varsity Basketball Team.

His love of *kī hōʻalu*, slack key guitar, led him to travel to Hawaiʻi and study with some of the masters. This in turn has led to a deep friendship with noted Hawaiian musician Keola Beamer and his illustrious family – Aunty Nona Beamer gave Mark his Hawaiian name, *Kailana,* which means "Gently Drifting on the Sea." Keola and Mark have collaborated on numerous projects, including a book, *Learn to Play Hawaiian Slack Key Guitar.* Together they host The Aloha Music Camp, a week-long immersion in the music and culture of Hawaiʻi held on the magical Island of Molokaʻi.

Mark lives in Southern Oregon's Applegate Valley with his wife Annie and various four-footed, winged and finny friends. He divides his time between studio work, writing, and watching the trees grow.

Selected Discography

The Water is Wide (Acme Arts 414K)
Slack Key Solos and Duets (Acme Arts)
Autumn (Wizmak Productions W579-33CD)
The Faery Hills (Wizmak Productions W579-34CD)
Southern Light (Flying Fish Records FF70405)
After the Morning (Kicking Mule Records KM 241)
The Rights of Man (Kicking Mule Records KM 218)

Books (Mel Bay Publications)

Learn to Play Hawaiian Slack Key Guitar (with Keola Beamer)
Advanced Concepts for Slack Key Guitar
Favorite Old-Time American Songs for Appalachian Dulcimer
The Complete Collection of Celtic Music for Appalachian Dulcimer
Scottish Airs and Ballads for Dulcimer

Contact Information
Mark Nelson
Acme Arts
PO Box 967
Jacksonville, OR 97530
www.Mark-o.com

Learn the 'ukulele in the land of its birth – Come to the Aloha Music Camp!
www.AlohaMusicCamp.com